DOIN'
DUTCH
OVEN

DOIN' DUTCH OVEN

Inside / and Out

ROBERT L. RIRIE

Cover Art by Patty Schafbuch

Sixth Printing: March 1999

International Standard Book Number
0-88290-368-3

Horizon Publishers' Catalog and Order Number
1218

Printed and distributed
in the United States of America by

Horizon Publishers
& Distributors, Incorporated

Mailing Address:
P.O. Box 490
Bountiful, Utah 84011-0490

Street Address:
50 South 500 West
Bountiful, Utah 84010

Phone and Fax:
Local Phone: (801) 295-9451
WATS (toll free): 1 (800) 453-0812
FAX: (801) 295-0196

Internet:
E-mail: horizonp@burgoyne.com
Home Page: http:// www.horizonpublishers.com

Table of Contents

Introduction

In my first book, *Let's Cook Dutch,* you were introduced to the world of Dutch oven cooking.

Those of you who hadn't done this type of cooking, or at the most had done very little, were taken beyond just the beginnings of Dutch oven art. As many of you wrote and told me, you tried lots of recipes you had not thought of in terms of this technique. In the book I went into how to season, clean, and take care of the great Dutch oven. I told you how to build fires conducive to cooking in them, and also told how to select the Dutch oven just right for your needs.

I received some great letters from people who really enjoyed using the first book. Thank you for taking the time to write and tell how much you like it.

So now that all of you who have the first book are great Dutch oven chefs, it's time to bring out the new book as promised.

In this volume I'll tell you about lots of new recipes. I'll tell you of the things that I have discovered to improve old ones. Many letters contained some tasty recipes. Some of the best ones will be included in a chapter called *Favorite Dutch Oven Recipes.*

There will also be a chapter on cooking in emergencies that will help all that want to be ready for any emergency in their family, whatever it might be, when they may have to cook meals away from microwave ovens, stoves, crockpots, etc.

The only limit on Dutch oven recipes is the limit of our imagination. There are a lot of outstanding recipes and ideas to help stimulate it. They'll make your mouth water, and you'll be able to give others help and advice on how to care for their families, too.

Cooking as a family is not only fun but good practice. It can be a good teaching experience for the kids who will be the Dutch oven chefs of the future. What better place for them to learn than from mom and dad. They might not be too thrilled at first, especially the younger ones, but teach what you can and remind them that someday they'll have families of their own to teach. When treated as something special for the whole family, they'll like it better and will enjoy the fun and good food all their life.

Also, one of the most important things I want to tell you is that you can cook indoors on your range or in your oven. Dutch oven cooking is not just for camping or for cookouts in the backyard.

The three legs on the Dutch oven fit over the electric or gas burner and work very well, as will putting a Dutch oven inside your oven. What this means is that you will be able to cook in your Dutch oven anytime you want a special dish or want to try something new. Even in winter you can enjoy it and you don't have to go outside and freeze. Remember, all these recipes can be cooked inside on your gas or electric range or in the oven and it is easy to regulate the heat. Keep it slow and easy.

Most people don't think about cooking indoors with a Dutch oven. But if they're like me, and love the taste of food cooked in Dutch ovens, they may want some of that special cooking even though it's cold or dark or just inconvenient to be out at the Bar-B-Q or Dutch oven pit in the backyard. If that's your problem, try it on your stove, both on top over the burners, or in the oven.

For example, all the frying can be done in a Dutch oven on top of your stove. Use it instead of a frying pan. Just put the size oven you need over a burner it will fit over. Almost all ranges have several sizes of burners. The three legs will keep it up over the burner (gas or electric). To brown the food, turn the heat up high, with lid off, and stand there to watch. Then, to simmer, put the lid on and turn down the heat. It will do a good job on all the recipes, as the flavor that cast-iron Dutch ovens give the food will be there. I think you'll be surprised at how good it will taste and what you can cook indoors with your Dutch ovens. It will be good for you people that live in snow country—you won't have to wait until spring to try some of these new ideas out. In the heat of summer, if you don't want to stand over a fire, cook indoors in your oven and turn your air conditioning down a little. A gas Bar-B-Q also works well if you don't want to heat up the house in summer.

I think this book is full of outstanding recipes and a lot of good ideas. Now that you've had the first book and over 10 years to practice, you should have all the confidence you need for more involved Dutch oven cooking. The effort will be worth it. So read on. Try them and enjoy!

I also must tell you that in this book, recipes for cooking on the stove or in the oven at home have temperature settings for electric ranges. So if you are using gas, please watch and adjust the heat so that you don't overcook your food or burn it. It's too good to waste! As an example, when I say start with high or medium high, that is so the heat from the burner will reach the bottom of the Dutch oven. The flame from gas will be closer to it, so start with medium heat and see what your stove will do. Remember, go slow and easy. Don't hurry your cooking. Give whatever you cook in a Dutch oven a chance to cook slowly and blend all the flavors in the juice.

One last comment before you get into the recipes. I like to use bacon grease to cook with in Dutch ovens. It gives a good flavor to any dish. I know it has cholesterol, and I'm not saying you have to cook with it for every meal, every day. Occasionally won't be so bad. If you have a high cholesterol level, don't use bacon grease—use a non-cholesterol vegetable oil and be careful with other foods with high cholesterol. You want to be around for a long time. Maybe a taste every once in awhile won't hurt you. I'm not telling you to eat all the cholesterol you want. All these recipes are very tasty, but for your health's sake, use good judgment in what you eat.

Now all you health-food people, please don't write me letters asking why I use bacon grease, sausage, ham, etc. in many of my recipes. It's because I like them. My cholesterol is low, and it sure is good to try all this great stuff once in awhile.

Dedication

This book is dedicated to my wife and family,

for their encouragement and help with the tasting

and testing of all my new recipes,

for all the good times we have had together,

and for all we will have.

Chapter One

Dutch Oven Appetizers and Dips

When you want a special appetizer or snack, try these. While watching a game on T.V., or when friends drop in and you want to have good food, that is when you'll enjoy these appetizers. You don't have to cook them in a Dutch oven, but I think everything tastes better cooked that way. See if you don't agree.

Dutch Oven Deep Fried Dogs

2 jumbo hot dogs per person
good vegetable oil—enough to cover a 12″ oven 1″ deep

Put a 12″ Dutch oven on stove top over a right-size burner. Pour oil in the Dutch oven. Put heat on high.

When the oil is hot, carefully place the cut hot dogs in the hot oil. Brown on both sides, turning them over with tongs. When brown and floating, remove with tongs or large slotted spoon. Put on paper towel to drain off excess oil. Press lightly with paper towel. Serve with one of the dips mentioned later in this chapter or one of your own favorite dips.

They will cook in about 10 minutes or less, depending on how many you are cooking.

I think you will be surprised at how good they are. Even my grandchildren like them. You can strain the oil back in the bottle and use it again, too.

Special Batter

For these next few special appetizers, I will give you the recipe for the batter and coating first, as it is used for all of them.

    4 eggs
    1 quart milk
    1 quart buttermilk
    seasoning

Blend together in bowl. If you are not cooking a lot, you can cut the recipe in half.

Special Breading

    2 cups fine bread crumbs
    2 cups cracker meal
    seasoning

If not cooking a lot, you can cut this recipe in half, too.
Blend the bread crumbs and cracker meal together in flat pan. Season to taste and blend it all again. You are now ready for my favorite appetizers or snacks, and you can make a meal of them if you want. I like them so much that I prepare them as a special lunch about once a week.

Dutch Oven Double-Dip Mushrooms

    good vegetable oil—at least 1½″ deep in Dutch oven
    button mushrooms—18 to 24 medium size

Will make bowl full for two people.
If you can't find the button mushrooms, buy the regular ones and break off the stems. Don't throw them away. Save to season another Dutch oven dish with.
Wash the mushrooms in cold water. Shake off excess water, then put them in the batter. Push down so they get coated all over. Remove with tongs and put in pan of coating mixture. Roll them in the crumbs,

then back in the batter, then back in the crumbs. Roll them again. They are now double dipped and ready for cooking.

On your stove top, have Dutch oven with the oil deep enough so the mushrooms can float. The oil has to be deeper than the mushrooms are in size. If you use large mushrooms, oil needs to be deeper than with small ones. Put the mushrooms in the oil to cook when oil is hot, on high. Cook until golden brown and floating. If it is too much of a coating for you, single dip them in batter, then the crumbs.

I love them both ways. I think you will, too. Serve in bowl lined with paper towel or napkin to absorb excess oil. Serve ranch dressing dip with them. Recipe in this chapter.

Dutch Oven Zucchini

1 zucchini per person
batter and coating as in the mushrooms

I like to slice my zucchini in ¼- to ½-inch slices, then put in batter, then in coating mix. You can double dip them if you want. Just repeat process in the batter, then in the coating.

If you like sticks of zucchini better than slices, cut in about 3″ pieces, then cut each 3″ piece in about 6-8 sticks. Put in batter mix, then coating mix. If you want double dipped, do it again.

Now cook them like the mushrooms cook—until golden brown and floating. It will take about 1½″ of oil if you don't make your sticks too big. Use high heat. If it gets too hot, use medium high. Put on paper towel to drain excess grease. Serve with ranch dressing dip, too.

Dutch Oven Onion Rings

Use large sweet white or red onions.

Use the center slices only—cut in as uniform a size as possible. I like mine about ¼″ thick. Save the rest of onion chopped up for other dishes. Now take the slices of onion, pull apart carefully and wash in cold water. Then put each slice in the batter, then the coating. I like my onion rings only dipped once, but you can do it double if you like them that way. If you are cooking a lot of them, put 2″ of oil in the Dutch oven on high to start. If too hot, turn down to medium high as with other appetizers. Cook until golden brown and floating. Remove with tongs. Put on paper towel to drain excess oil.

Fix about 12 onion rings per person. Serve with ranch dressing dip or whatever you like with them.

A couple of things before we go on. When the crumb coating mix has lumps in it, strain them out. Add more if needed and you can save it for use again.

Same with the batter mix. Strain it and you can use it again, too. But keep in refrigerator. It will not keep as long as the dry crumbs do, so try to use it all and make new batter each time.

For those of you that don't like any of these appetizers, or have never had them cooked in a Dutch oven, you sure missed a very good treat. Even when it is this much work they are worth it every time I make them. Try them and see before you think it's too hard or too much trouble.

A couple of things before we go on. When the crumb coating mix has lumps in it, strain them out. Add more if needed and you can save it for use again.

Same with the batter mix. Strain it and you can use it again, too. But keep in refrigerator. It will not keep as long as the dry crumbs do, so try to use it all and make new batter each time.

For those of you that don't like any of these appetizers, or have never had them cooked in a Dutch oven, you sure missed a very good treat. Even when it is this much work they are worth it every time I make them. Try them and see before you think it's too hard or too much trouble.

Chapter Two

Chicken Wings

Chicken wings are very popular. They don't cost much, they taste very good, and they are a good snack or side dish. I think they taste better cooked in a Dutch oven. So in this chapter, I'll tell you the ways I like them best. You try them and see if I am right.

The Chicken Wings Supreme are the best I have ever tasted. All the other recipes are good too, so you can choose how you like them best.

Dutch Oven Quickie Chicken Wings

12 wings per person, cut at joint (no wing tips)
vegetable oil to cover oven 1″ deep
seasoning

On top of stove, put your Dutch oven over right-size burner. Add oil. Put heat on high. When oil is hot, put in wings. Cook until brown and tender. If too hot, use medium high heat. They then can be taken out with tongs and put on paper towels to remove excess oil. Then season to taste and dip in your favorite dip. Mine is Ranch Dressing Dip or Bar-B-Q sauce.

Dutch Oven Quickie Wings in Bar-B-Q Sauce

12 wings per person
6 tbsp. bacon grease or vegetable oil
seasoning
1 lg. bottle hickory smoked Bar-B-Q sauce

On your stove top, place the Dutch oven over right-size burner. Put in bacon grease. Turn to high long enough to brown all the wings. Have the wings, cut at joint, seasoned to taste and put in the hot grease. Turn until all brown. Reduce heat to medium. Add hickory smoked Bar-B-Q sauce. Simmer with lid on Dutch oven until tender (about 30-40 minutes depending on how many you are cooking). When tender take out and place in bowl. You can use sauce to dip them in.

If you have a recipe for your own Bar-B-Q sauce, use it. If not, try the one on page 38 of *Let's Cook Dutch*. If in a hurry, use a good grade of hickory flavor Bar-B-Q sauce. If you like yours hot, add teaspoons of tabasco, one at a time, until hot enough for your taste.

Also, for more than 48 wings, you might need more bacon grease for browning and more than 1 large bottle of hickory smoked Bar-B-Q sauce. But you knew that, right?

Now a couple more ways to cook chicken wings.

Dutch Oven Oriental Chicken Wings

¼ cup flour	2 cloves garlic—crushed
½ cup cornstarch	3 eggs—lightly beaten
¼ cup sugar	48 chicken wings (for 4 people)
1 tsp. salt or to taste	2 tbsp. bacon grease or
2 tbsp. soy sauce	vegetable oil
¼ cup chopped onion	seasoning

In a large bowl, combine flour, cornstarch, sugar, salt, soy sauce, chopped onions, garlic and eggs. Mix it well, add chicken wings, and marinate 3 to 4 hours.

When ready to start cooking, put Dutch oven on right-size burner. Turn to high and add bacon grease. Season wings to taste, then put in Dutch oven and brown. When browned, turn heat down to medium. Pour the marinade over the wings. Put lid on and cook until tender. Or, you can also put in oven on 250 to 300 degrees. Cook until tender. Use the sauce as the dip for the wings.

Good eating! Serves 4 (12 each). You can make them hot by adding tabasco as you like it.

Dutch Oven Sweet and Sour Chicken Wings

½ cup vinegar
1 cup water
1 cup catsup
½ cup sugar
¼ tsp. salt or to taste
2 tsp. soy sauce
2 tsp. cornstarch
48 chicken wings for 4
2 tbsp. bacon grease or vegetable oil
seasoning

Put Dutch oven on right-size burner on medium high. Put bacon grease in the Dutch oven while getting hot. Season wings to taste. When grease is hot, brown the wings. When brown, turn down to medium low, put on lid and make sweet and sour sauce.

To make sweet and sour sauce, combine vinegar, water, catsup, sugar, salt and soy sauce in saucepan and heat on medium. Mix cornstarch with a small amount of water to make a paste to stir into sauce. Cook and stir sweet and sour sauce until smooth, transparent and thickened, but so it will pour.

Then take lid off Dutch oven. Pour sauce over chicken wings. Put heat on medium. Cook until tender. Stir them up a couple of times. These are good, too.

I don't know about you, but I like chicken wings as a snack or side dish and all of these are worth the trouble it takes to fix them. So if you have not been a chicken wing fan, try them for yourself and see what you have been missing.

There are other ways to cook chicken wings, but these are the ones I like best and the next recipe is my favorite.

Dutch Oven Chicken Wings Supreme

6-12 chicken wings per person
2 tbsp. vegetable oil or bacon grease
seasoning you like
1 cup flour or more if large amount of chicken
1 paper bag

Chicken wings are a good snack and they can be a special treat. If you like wings you will love these. I think they are the best I have ever tasted. I hope you like them, too.

Depending on how many you are going to cook, select the right size Dutch oven. If you are doing it inside on the stove select the right size burner too, so that the Dutch oven will sit on the outside of the burner on its three legs. Now you are ready to start.

Take paper bag, put in the flour and seasoning. Then add the chicken wings a few at a time and shake them in the bag so the seasoned flour will cover them. With a set of tongs, remove chicken from sack and shake off excess flour. Repeat until all wings are floured.

Heat the Dutch oven on medium high, add bacon grease or vegetable oil. When hot, brown all the wings, one layer at a time until all are brown. You can pile them on one side of the oven or use a separate oven to keep them warm on another burner.

When the chicken wings are all brown, put them in the Dutch oven in layers. Be sure there is at least ¼″ of oil in the bottom of the Dutch oven to insure the sauce not burning. Pour the special sauce (recipe below) over them.

INDOORS
Put Dutch oven in oven with lid on and bake at 300° for 45

minutes or until tender to the fork. Try not to overcook them or they will fall apart. They still taste great, but are hard to pick up.

OUTDOORS
Be sure to have most of your heat on top. Also, be sure to stir the wings approximately every 10 minutes to insure even cooking.

Special Sauce for Chicken Wings

¼ cup soy sauce
½ cup sugar
½ cup vinegar
1 cup barbecue sauce
¼ cup water

Blend all together in a large cup or bowl to pour over wings after they are browned and before they go into the oven. If you like them hot add 2 tbsp. tabasco sauce.

Ranch Dip

1 pkg. Ranch House mix (season to taste)
1 quart buttermilk
1 quart sour cream

Mix well and you have a good dip. If this is too much, cut in half. It will still make a quart. The Ranch House mix has all the spices in it and will be in the salad dressing section of the grocery store.
This is the dip I like best. Some like the Thousand Island dip. These are the ones I use for chicken wings, mushrooms, onion rings, etc. If you have a favorite dip recipe, try it too.

Thousand Island Dip

1½ cups mayonnaise
½ cup catsup
¼ cup sweet relish
salt and pepper to taste

Mix all together and you have another dip to try.

For more dips that go with appetizers and snack foods, see the chapter on Complementary Side Dishes. You can also use the sauces from the chicken wings. Just make extra Bar-B-Q sauce, sweet and sour, and oriental. All are good for dipping appetizers.

Chapter Three

Dutch Oven Breakfast Specials

In this group of breakfast special treats, you will find the ones I like best. You can cook them in your oven at home, in the outdoors with briquettes, or in your fireplace with coals. Any way you try them, I think you will find out they are special, so don't be afraid to give them a try.

Dutch Oven Drop Biscuits

2 cups sifted all-purpose flour
3 tbsp. baking powder
½ tsp. salt
⅓ cup shortening
1 cup milk

Sift dry ingredients, flour, baking powder and salt into bowl. Blend in the shortening with a fork until dough goes around bowl, then dump out onto lightly floured cutting board. Knead gently 12 strokes, then spoon into Dutch oven.

A 12″ Dutch oven will hold 12 of them. If you want to make a double batch, double the recipe and use a 14″ Dutch oven.

INDOORS
Put in regular oven with lid off. Bake at 450° for 10-12 minutes.

OUTDOORS
The lid must be placed on the Dutch oven and most of the heat must be on the lid in order to bake the biscuits and not burn them.
Now you have the biscuits down, let's try some other good stuff.

Dutch Oven Milk Gravy

milk (1 cup per person)
flour as needed to thicken (should be mixed with water
    to avoid unnecessary lumps)
seasoning (salt and pepper)
1 cup chopped bacon or sausage (optional)

If cooking indoors on stove, use a 10- or 12-inch Dutch oven, depending upon how much you are cooking. Now cook the bacon or sausage until browned. Make sure it is in small pieces. Leave bacon or sausage pieces in the Dutch oven with grease. Add the milk, season to taste. Turn heat to medium high so milk will boil. Keep stirring milk and add flour and water mixture to thicken the way you like it.

I like mine with both bacon and sausage, and the gravy so it will pour. It is very important to keep stirring the gravy all the time so that it will not burn. A whip will work best, but a spoon will do the job.

If you like gravy over biscuits as I do, you may want to make extra. I can't tell you what to do if any is left over. I have never had any left, but I am sure it could be saved and used the next day.

If cooking this gravy while out camping, do the same, but watch heat as it will be harder to keep the heat regulated. Stir it all the time and don't get it hotter than you need. It will be a very special treat wherever you use it.

Pour the gravy over the biscuits, pigs in a blanket or whatever you made it for. You will see why this is one of my favorite breakfasts. I even like it for lunch or supper.

Dutch Oven Eggs Goldenrod

hard boiled eggs (2 per adult, 1 per child)
milk (1 cup per person)
flour as needed to thicken (should be mixed with water
    to avoid unnecessary lumps)
seasoning (salt and pepper)
1 cup chopped bacon or sausage (optional)

Make the gravy the same as in the "Dutch Oven Milk Gravy" recipe except now you do something special. Peel the shell off the hard-boiled eggs, remove the yolks and keep separate. Chop up or grate the egg whites into the finished milk gravy. Take the egg yolks and grate or chop them up very fine. Put them into a bowl.

When you are ready to eat, spoon the gravy over the biscuits, pigs in a blanket or anything you choose. Then, for that final special touch, spoon on the egg yolk. This is really a very special treat. Hope you like it as much as we do.

All of these breakfast recipes go well together and complement each other. But biscuits and gravy will sure perk up the old standby ham and eggs, bacon and eggs, etc. And don't be afraid to throw in some leftover Dutch oven potatoes as hash browns. You can make a lot of special breakfasts at home or out camping, so try them out and see what you can come up with.

Dutch Oven Pigs in a Blanket

If you have your own biscuit recipe, use it or the one given previously. In a separate Dutch oven, cook the sausage links (or sausage patties, if you prefer them). I like both and will use whichever is handy. Now, back to the cooking.

Brown the sausages on both sides (or all around, if links), but do not overcook them, just brown them. When brown, remove from the Dutch oven and blot on paper towels. Try to leave a little grease and a little sausage in the Dutch oven for the milk gravy we talked about before.

With the biscuit recipe take one large spoonful of the dough and wrap around each sausage link. Place it in a clean Dutch oven to bake. Continue until all sausage links are covered.

If you are using sausage patties, put one spoonful of dough on the board, put in patty, and place another spoon of dough on top. Fold in edges and put in a clean Dutch oven. This will make 6 large or 12 small. Cook the same as biscuits, at 450° for 10-12 minutes. They may take a little longer than 12 minutes, but watch them. Do not overcook.

Chapter Four

Dutch Oven Chili and Special Beans

Dutch Oven Chili Without Beans

2 lbs. lean coarse ground beef
2 lbs. lean beef (cut in small pieces)
4 large onions—chopped
1 clove garlic
1 large green pepper
¼ cup bacon grease or vegetable oil
3 tbsp. flour
1 oz. ground cumin
3 oz. chili powder
4 cups boiling water
2 tbsp. black pepper
2 tbsp. red pepper
2 tbsp. season salt
1 tbsp. garlic powder

Put 14″ Dutch oven on large burner on top of the stove. Set on medium heat. Put bacon grease or vegetable oil in pan. Add lean beef pieces and brown on all sides. When completely brown, add the coarse ground beef and continue to brown until all of the pink color is gone. Add the chopped onion, garlic and green pepper. Mix in well.

Put lid on the Dutch oven and let simmer. While meat mixture is cooking, mix in a separate bowl the following: boiling water, cumin and chili powder. Pour over meat mixture and stir in well. If the mixture is too thick, add a bit more water to make it a medium consistency. Let simmer on low for a couple of hours, stirring every once in awhile to keep it from sticking and burning. After approximately two hours, spoon off the excess grease, let it simmer longer. The longer you let it cook, the better it is going to taste—3 to 4 hours usually does the trick.

This recipe makes 15 to 20 bowls of chili.

Also, this is not a "hot" chili. If you like it hot, add two jalapeno peppers with the seeds taken out and chopped up. Add this along with the onions, pepper and garlic. Also, 1 tbsp. of tabasco sauce will give it the hot flavor.

Dutch ovens seem to make all the foods taste better. This makes a good chili that can be saved and eaten the next day. Or freeze it for use another day when you know you won't have the time to fix something this good.

Just because this recipe was given for indoor cooking doesn't mean it can't be used outdoors. Just remember, slow and easy for most of the day, for suppertime you will have a special treat.

For a special taste delight, sprinkle grated cheese over the hot bowl of chili just before you serve it.

Dutch Oven Chili with Polish Sausage

1 piece Polish sausage per person
1 cup chili per person
chopped onion, sweet
grated cheese
2 tbsp. bacon grease or vegetable oil
seasoning

If you ever have leftover chili and don't want to eat it plain, boy, have I got a treat for you! You can fix it on top of the stove at home or over a campfire or briquettes.

Put the Dutch oven on the heat. Put in bacon grease or vegetable oil. Brown the Polish sausages on all sides (stovetop, use medium heat). Brown them slowly. When brown, add chili and mix it all together. Turn heat down to medium low. Put lid on Dutch oven. Cook slowly for 15-20 minutes. Spoon out the sausage in individual bowls. Put the chili on top. Add the grated cheese and then chopped onions. Serve with corn bread or hot rolls. That is good eating!

I like mine best with the beanless chili (recipe in this book), but any kind will do. I have even used canned chili. It's good, too. Also, you can use the jumbo hot dogs, summer sausage or whatever you like—they are all good. Try them for a quick treat.

One last tip. Whenever you make up a batch of chili, make extra and freeze it. Then when you go camping or want to try it, all you need to do is defrost the chili and go for it. It is so good, you will want to make extra.

Bob's Special Waltz Beans

½ lb. bacon
1 lb. lean ground beef
½ lb. ground sausage
1 15-oz. can oven baked beans
1 15-oz. can kidney beans
1 15-oz. can pinto beans
1 cup catsup
1 tbsp. worcestershire sauce
1 tbsp. vinegar
1 large onion—chopped fine
1 large green pepper—chopped fine
1 tbsp. bottled mustard
1 tbsp. brown sugar
salt and pepper for seasoning

If cooking *INSIDE* place Dutch oven on top of stove. Brown the bacon, then add onions and peppers and brown them. When browned add ground beef and sausage. Brown meat well, then drain off the excess grease. Season meat to your taste. Mix in all the remaining ingredients. Put lid on Dutch oven and put in the oven at 350° for one hour. This time will allow all the flavors to blend together. I like mine served with some grated cheese on top. These are some of the best beans I have ever eaten, so cook plenty.

This will serve 8-10 people. If you need to serve more, double the recipe.

After you try them you will want to cook them *OUTSIDE* camping, too. Remember to have heat on the bottom only until the meat is browned. After adding all the ingredients and mixing them well, put the lid on and add heat to the top of the Dutch oven. It might take a little longer, but don't burn them by adding too much heat. It's a good idea, outdoors, to stir them to see how they are cooking. Then you can see if you need more heat, less heat, or if they're doing fine. They will be worth the time it will take. I have had people eat these that said they don't generally like beans. So don't worry about leftovers.

A last tip: if you like your beans spicy hot, in addition to the green pepper, you can add hot peppers or one or more teaspoons of tabasco sauce.

This can be a main dish or served as a side dish with ribs, roast, meat loaf, steaks or whatever, but do try them when you want something special. These beans also make a special treat when put over biscuits with sausage in them.

Adapted from a recipe given to me by some special friends, Mr. and Mrs. Glen Alleman of Las Vegas, Nevada and Springville, Utah.

Waltz Bean Chili

These beans are so good. To make a quick chili, just add one large tablespoon of chili powder and one large can of tomato juice when you add all the other ingredients. After the meat is browned, stir in and let simmer, or you can add the chili powder and tomato juice to any leftover beans. Let simmer until warm and you have a very good quick chili with leftovers. We try to have some left over just to make into this chili, so try it too, on your next batch.

Dutch Oven Ham and Beans

ham hocks
small ham cut in pieces
lima beans (baby or regular), 1 lb. pkg. will feed
    about 8-10 people
1 large onion—chopped fine
optional—garlic, green pepper

After the beans have soaked for a couple of hours (3-4 hours is all I soak mine), put the ham hocks in about 2 quarts of water with the onion (the garlic and green pepper too, if you desire). Cook for about 1 hour and then add the extra ham. By now the soaking beans should be ready.

Drain the lima beans and add to the Dutch oven ham that is already cooking. Season to taste. Mix thoroughly and let simmer for 2 hours.

Remember to test the beans so they will be cooked just the way you like them. If you like your beans very soft, you may want to add ½ hour to the cooking time.

As the Dutch oven gives everything a better flavor, try this bean recipe next time you are in the mood for beans. Until I worked up the "Special Beans," this recipe was my favorite and I still enjoy it.

You can cook these beans on the range or out camping. Remember, the secret is to slow cook them until they are the way you like them.

Serve these beans with cornbread, which is my favorite, or with biscuits.

Dutch Oven Special 15 Beans with Ham

I love ham and beans, and in a Dutch oven, they are even better, and these are better yet. Everyone has a regular recipe for ham and beans and I have given you mine, but this is a special mix that you will like, too.

> ham hocks and small pieces of ham cut into
>   bite-size pieces
> 1 pkg. 15 bean mix
> 1 large chopped onion
> 1 large can tomatoes
> 1 tsp. chili powder
> 1 clove minced garlic
> 1 tsp. lemon juice
> seasoning (salt and pepper)
> optional: hot peppers, tabasco sauce

Take the package of 15 beans and wash thoroughly, place in a pan and cover with water. Add 2 tbsp. of salt and let soak overnight. When you are ready to start cooking them, drain the beans and add 2 quarts of water and pour into the Dutch oven. Add the ham and/or ham hocks. Let simmer for 2 to 2½ hours. Stir once in awhile and don't let it get too hot.

While the beans are cooking have the onion chopped, the clove of garlic minced and add them to the beans with the tomatoes, chili powder, lemon juice, and hot peppers if you desire. Salt and pepper to taste. Let simmer 30-45 minutes.

Just a few minutes before you're ready to eat the beans, add the seasoning packet to the beans, mix in and let simmer for a couple of minutes.

This can be served with crackers or my favorite, cornbread. This will feed about 12 people, and if there is any left over it is great the next day, too.

One more thing: the longer you soak the beans, the softer they get. The same thing goes for cooking them, so if you want your beans firm, don't soak overnight; maybe 4 hours will be enough. I like mine soft, but not mush, so regular beans I soak about 4 hours, mixed beans a little longer because some of them are harder than others.

Do try these beans—they are some of the best ham and beans I have ever eaten.

Adapted from a recipe given to me by Wanda Galen, Las Vegas.

Dutch Oven Tortilla Chips and Beans

Use the bean recipe on page 55 of *Let's Cook Dutch,* or use one of the following bean recipes in this section: Bob's Special Waltz Beans or Special 15 Beans with Ham.

    1 package tortilla chips
    1 cup grated cheese

When all ingredients are mixed put them in the oven at 350° for 30-45 minutes. Remove from oven and take off the Dutch oven lid. Cover top of beans with tortilla chips and cheese. Put in oven at 300° for another 15 minutes or until cheese is melted. When cheese is melted it's ready to eat. You can eat it with a fork or scoop up with the tortilla chips.

If cooking outdoors, watch heat. Cooking time will be a little longer, just keep your eyes on the beans. Stir once in a while so you can see how they are cooking. I like to taste everything, I stir so I can tell how they are doing. This is a little bonus about being the cook, I get to sample all of the good stuff when it's cooking.

I love these, I hope you do, too. You can use corn chips if no tortilla chips are available.

Chapter Five

Dutch Oven Casseroles

Casseroles are a good way to have a complete good-tasting meal. I think they can be very good eating when cooked in a Dutch oven instead of a crock pot or baking dish. The Dutch oven gives them more flavor. I have included my favorite ones in this section. There are, of course, a lot of others I have tried that are good, too.

Try your favorite casserole adapted to a Dutch oven in the house on top of your stove and then in the oven slow and easy. If it doesn't work one way, try another. There are several hundred casserole recipes around. I keep trying new ones all the time. It is fun to work up a recipe. You can have fun doing it, too. Practice makes perfect. By now if you have been doing a lot of Dutch oven cooking, you can think through it and try what you think will work. It probably will—if not, change what didn't work and go on.

The recipes in this section will give you some good ideas and a place to start. Good luck and enjoy eating the good casseroles you will cook.

Dutch Oven Chicken with Rice

1 chicken breast per person
½ cup cooked rice per person
1 can mushroom soup
1 cup milk
1 can sliced mushrooms
½ cup bacon grease
1 tbsp. salt
1 tbsp. pepper
1 tbsp. seasoning salt
1 tbsp. garlic salt

If cooking outside, get your coals ready and put on the Dutch oven. Add the bacon grease. When hot put in the chicken breasts and brown on both sides. Put the lid of the oven on and add briquettes or coals to the top, let simmer until tender (35 to 45 minutes). If you are cooking a lot, it may take an hour.

While chicken is browning, prepare the rice. There are a lot of quick and easy brands on the market, so if you don't want to go to the trouble of waiting for long-cooking rice, use one of those. When the chicken is tender and done, remove oven from the heat and let cool until you can easily bone the chicken. Keep all of the juice from the chicken in the oven. When the chicken is boned, put a layer of rice in the bottom of the oven. Mix this up with the juice and add the seasonings. Place the chicken over the rice. Mix the mushroom soup and the milk together and pour over the chicken and the rice.

Now the reason you have had the oven off of the coals is so you can remove most of the coals from the bottom and place the heat on the lid. You're going to bake it, not boil it. Leave about 6 or 7 briquettes and replace oven. Add 12 to 15 briquettes to the top and let bake for 20 minutes until sauce has worked its way down into the chicken and rice mixture and it is hot.

If you add a small package of frozen peas to the rice when you place it in the oven, you won't have to worry about serving a vegetable with this dish. It will already be in there.

Now, if you are cooking inside, the techniques are a little different. Place the oven over the burner that is closest to the size of the oven you are using. Turn to high. Add bacon grease and brown the chicken, then turn the burner heat down to medium and let simmer until done. Follow the same instructions for boning, rice, and mushroom sauce. Then place the Dutch oven into oven, with the temperature set at 300° for 20 minutes until hot and bubbly.

Options:

You can use any chicken part that you want to. I have found that it is easier to bone the breasts. This is important: get out all of the bones, no one wants to bite down on one.

You can also use this recipe for any other fowl: quail, mourning dove, pheasant, or even rabbit.

If you don't want to leave the breasts whole, cut them in bite-size pieces after you bone them.

Any way that you decide to fix it, you are going to be surprised at how good it is. It's one of our grandchildren's very favorites.

Dutch Oven Chicken Creole

A few tips and ideas before we get down to the recipe. First, you can use any piece of chicken, or the whole chicken cut up in pieces if you like. Figure on 1 chicken for every 2 adults. If you are using specific pieces use 1-2 chicken breasts per person or 3-5 legs or thighs. If you know everyone's eating habits, judge how much chicken you will need to cook.

1 frying chicken for 2 people
1 large onion
1 large green pepper
1 can drained stewed tomatoes
¼ cup bacon grease or vegetable oil
1 cup milk
2 eggs
1 cup flour
salt and pepper for seasoning
garlic powder

Mix the eggs up in the milk. This is the batter. Cut up the chicken or use the pieces you have chosen. Dip the chicken pieces in the batter and then in the flour. When the Dutch oven is hot, brown all the chicken as quickly as you can. Keep the Dutch oven on high until all the chicken is browned. Drain off extra grease.

Now place layers of chicken in Dutch oven alternately with layers of onions and peppers. Season with garlic powder and salt and pepper to taste. Repeat until all chicken, onions and peppers are used. Pour the tomatoes over it all and season to taste.

INDOORS
Bake at 325-350° in your oven for 1 to 1½ hours. The more you cook, the more time it will take, but you should be done in about 1½ hours.

OUTDOORS
If cooking out camping, keep most of the heat on top as you are baking it. It might take a little longer, but most of the time it will cook in 1½ hours, too. Keep an eye on it.

One last tip. If you're willing to go to a little more trouble, use boneless breasts—they won't be dry. If you like hot food, add hot peppers or tabasco to heat it up.

Adapted from a recipe given to me by Lea Estep, Las Vegas.

Dutch Oven Apache-Pino Meat with Rice

If you are wondering about the name, I have a niece that is ½ Apache and ½ Philippino and she calls herself Apache-Pino. Since this recipe is adapted from one of hers, I named this recipe after her.

> ½ lb. boneless meat per person
> 3 cups vinegar
> 2 cups water
> ½ bottle soy sauce
> ¼ cup bacon grease or vegetable oil
> seasoning (salt and pepper) to taste
> 1 cup cooked rice per person

Cut meat into small pieces and cut off excess fat.

If cooking this inside, put Dutch oven on top of stove on medium high. Add bacon grease or vegetable oil. While it is getting hot, season meat to taste, then brown it. When brown on all sides, drain off all the grease, pour in the vinegar, water and soy sauce, put in the oven at 250° and cook until tender. Look at it and stir up at least once. It will take 40-60 minutes for a normal batch. If cooking a lot, it will take longer, as you know.

Serve over the rice.

Other ideas: you can use any kind of meat (beef, pork, or lamb).

If cooking outside, when browning, have the heat on the bottom of the Dutch oven. Then when all the meat is browned, put most of the heat on the top to bake it. Cooking time will be longer. Watch it carefully and don't let it cook all the juice out and burn.

You can use fried rice instead of boiled rice if you prefer.

If you don't like soy sauce, try it this way. Use your favorite gravy or sauce over the meat and rice, such as mushroom, or chicken. Experiment and you will be surprised at how good it is.

Dutch Oven Hungarian Goulash

2 lbs. boneless beef—cut in 1-inch cubes
⅓ cup flour
2 tbsp. bacon grease or vegetable oil
1 cup water
½ cup chopped onions
2 tbsp. catsup
2 tsp. beef bouillon granules
1 tsp. paprika
2-3 bay leaves
seasoning

For Sauce
3 tbsp. all-purpose flour
½ cup sour cream

Season the cut-up beef roast to taste. Then, in a plastic bag add ⅓ cup flour and then the beef. Shake well to coat it all over. On top of the stove on medium high, put meat in the Dutch oven to brown with whatever you are using (2 tbsp. bacon grease or vegetable oil). When meat is browned, carefully stir in 1 cup water, chopped onions, catsup, beef bouillon granules, paprika, and bay leaves. Put lid on Dutch oven and put in oven on 250 degrees. Cook until tender (about 2½ hours). Check it until it is the way you like your meat. Remove the meat when tender. Keep warm. Put Dutch oven back on top of the stove over medium high until liquid starts to boil. Remove bay leaves, then take out in a separate bowl, 1 cup of the hot cooking liquid. Mix in the flour and sour cream slowly, then pour into the Dutch oven. Put meat back in. Turn heat down low while you get the noodles or rice ready. Serve over buttered noodles or rice and rolls or french bread. Goulash is a good meal, but this way it seems better.

Now a couple of hints. If you use a good cut of meat (like tri tip or sirloin tip), it will cook tender faster, but you can also use chuck or any boneless beef. Just remember, cook low until tender. It might take longer, but it will be worth it.

If out camping and you want to try it, just allow time to cook it slowly, with most of the heat on top after meat has browned.

This recipe will serve 6 so you will know how to plan the amount you will cook.

Dutch Oven Chicken/ Sausage Casserole

1 boneless chicken breast per person
½ pound pork sausage for every 4 breasts
½ cup carrot—finely chopped
½ cup celery—finely chopped
½ cup onion—finely chopped
1½ cup tomato juice
1 tbsp. Worcestershire sauce
2 tsp. beef bouillon
½ tsp. basil—dried and crushed
½ tsp. oregano—dried and crushed
½ tsp. paprika
seasoning

On top of the stove, set the heat for medium high. Brown the sausage lightly with the carrots, celery and onions. Season to taste, then remove the excess grease. Season and brown the boneless chicken breasts. Turn the heat off. Add tomato juice, Worcestershire sauce, beef bouillon, basil, oregano, and paprika.

Now put the Dutch oven, with lid on, in the oven on 250 degrees. Cook until tender, for 2-3 hours depending on how big the breasts are and how many you cook.

When tender, put a chicken breast over a serving of rice or potatoes and pour the juice from the Dutch oven over each one. Serve while hot with the side dish of your choice.

Options: You can use any chicken you like, but boneless works better. It will be hard to get the meat off the bone in the juice if boneless chicken is not used. You can also use sliced Polish sausage instead of bulk sausage—it's good, too. Also, when you check and it's about done, if the chicken is low on juice, add a little more tomato juice.

You can probably think of other ways to try it, so go for it. This one is good and your idea will be, too.

Marie's Mexican Lasagna

1½ lb. ground beef
1 tsp. seasoned salt
1 pkg. (1¼ oz.) taco seasoning
1 cup (8 oz.) diced canned tomatoes
2 cans (8 oz. ea.) tomato sauce
1 can (4 oz.) chopped green chilies
8 oz. ricotta cheese
2 eggs
9 corn tortillas
10 oz. Monterey jack cheese

Place ground beef in a 12″ Dutch oven. Brown ground beef until crumbly. Drain fat by tipping the Dutch oven to the side and removing excess fat with a large spoon. Add seasoned salt, taco mix, tomatoes, tomato sauce and chilies. Simmer uncovered 10 minutes. Combine ricotta cheese and eggs.

Remove half of the ground beef mixture and set aside. Top the remaining half of the meat mixture with half the corn tortillas. Spread half the ricotta cheese mixture over tortillas and top with half the grated jack cheese. Repeat the layers once more, ending with grated jack cheese.

INDOORS:
Bake at 350° for 20-30 minutes.

OUTDOORS:
Put most of the heat on top (18-20 briquettes) and a few on the bottom (4-5).

Let stand 10 minutes before cutting.
Serves 4 hungry people or 8 polite people.

Paula's Chili Relleno Casserole

1 lb. ground beef
½ cup onion—chopped
½ tsp. salt
¼ tsp. pepper
1 small can whole chilies
½ cup grated cheese

1½ cup milk
¼ cup flour
pinch pepper
4 eggs beaten

Brown the beef and onion in the Dutch oven, drain the grease and add seasoning. Place chilies over the ground beef, then cheese.

Beat the remaining ingredients and pour over chilies, meat and cheese.

INDOORS:
Bake without lid for 45 minutes at 350°

OUTDOORS:
Place most of the heat on the lid. Cook until the top of the casserole is firm. Check after 20 minutes.

A recipe from my daughter, Paula.

Chapter Six

Dutch Oven Special Hot Dogs

Dutch Oven Baked Dough Dogs

In *Let's Cook Dutch,* pages 59-61, I told you about a couple of simple dishes with the lowly hot dog as the main item. With this book, I told you about the appetizers. Now, as with all recipes in this book, here is something a little more involved but well worth it.

> 2 dogs per person, 1 for children
> (use large dogs 8 per package)
> 1 slice of cheese for each (for inside of hot dog—
> the choice of cheese is up to you)
> *Optional:* 1 sucker or popsicle stick for each

First, prepare your dough. If you don't have a recipe, use the one in *Let's Cook Dutch,* page 85, or use a package of bread or roll dough. In the packaged bread section of your market there are several varieties of bread or roll dough. Just pick out the kind you like, as it is ready to use. It will be quicker and will work fine.

Roll out a large-enough piece of dough to cover the hot dogs out to the end, and wide enough to roll them up in. When the dough is ready, take the large premium hot dogs and cut them on one side. Put in enough cheese to fill up the cut. If you prefer, sprinkle cheese on both sides of the hot dog without slicing it. Roll the hot dog up in the dough and place in the Dutch oven on a rack.

INDOORS:

Bake at 300° for 15 to 20 minutes or until brown. Do not put the lid on so the biscuits won't burn on the bottom.

OUTDOORS:
Do not get the oven too hot, and keep most of the heat on the top. Cook until brown.

When brown, remove from the oven with tongs or gloves as they will be hot. Now, if you want to, you can insert the sucker stick in one end. Then dip in catsup, mustard or a good salsa dip.

One more thing, if you don't like or can't eat cheese, they are very good without it.

Try them!

Dutch Oven Special
Stuffed Hot Dogs

1 or 2 jumbo dogs per person
1 or 2 pieces of bacon per dog (thick cut)
sliced cheese

This is a quick treat—the kids love them, too.

First, in the Dutch oven, cook the bacon on medium. Do not cook until crisp, as you will have to wrap it around the dogs later. Cook it so it will bend without breaking. After the bacon is ready, remove it from the oven.

Brown the dogs on all sides still on medium. Cook them slowly to keep the juice in. When brown, turn off the heat. Remove the dogs with tongs and cut a slice down the middles, starting and ending ½ inch from each end. Now stuff in the sliced cheese. Then wrap the bacon around the dogs and hold with toothpicks at the ends of the bacon. When all wrapped, put back in the Dutch oven with cheese stuffing on top. Put the lid on the Dutch oven and put in your oven at 225 or 250 degrees for 5 to 8 minutes until cheese melts—then they are ready to eat. (Remove the toothpicks before you eat them.)

This recipe is good for a quick lunch just plain, or with beans or chili on a hot dog bun. I like them all ways, even just the way they come out of the Dutch oven. They're a very simple way to have a good quick meal. You can also put chili over them, add some chopped onions and hot corn bread, and it's a good main course. Give them a try. See what you can do with the lowly hot dog and a Dutch oven.

Chapter Seven

Favorite Dutch Oven Recipes

In this chapter I will be passing on to you some recipes that were sent to me. I hope you try them when you can. The directions and contents are just as I received them. My comments or suggestions will follow each recipe.

Dutch Oven French Dressing Chicken

Take chicken cut in pieces. Remove the skin. Layer in a 12" Dutch oven. On the first layer pour some French dressing. Sprinkle with dry onion soup mix. Spread orange marmalade or apricot jam over this. Place another layer of chicken on top and repeat above process until the oven is full.

Usually legs and thighs are used for this—about 15 in a 12" Dutch oven. Takes one large bottle of French dressing, one package of dry onion soup mix, and one medium size jar of jam. Takes approximately 1 hour to cook. You can use the juice from the chicken to pour over rice as a side dish.

Author's Note: No temperature was included, but if indoor in oven, cook at 300 degrees for one hour. Check it—when tender to fork it's done. If outdoors, use about 16 to 18 briquettes on top and 6 to 8 on the bottom. It will still cook in about 1 hour.

From Charles Conn, Carlsbad, California

Dutch Oven Ground Steak Patties

2 lbs. ground steak
1 large bell pepper—chopped
1 large onion—chopped
small amount of flour

1 can cream of mushroom soup

Mix the first 4 ingredients together and form into 4 patties. Brown these in the Dutch oven and then pour the can of cream of mushroom soup over them. Bake for 30 minutes. Use about 32 briquettes, with 25 on top and 7 on the bottom.

Author's Note: He didn't say about cooking it indoors. In your oven at home, set it at about 300 degrees. Cook for 30 minutes longer if you want it cooked well. Here again, cook it long enough to be as you like it. Also, the size of the oven is not listed. In a 12" Dutch oven you can put 4 patties if not too flattened. If you want to make them larger, or make more than 4 of them, use a 14" oven. The thinner the patty, they faster they cook.

From Olaos Njos, McIntosh, South Dakota

Dutch Oven Broccoli Casserole

3 10 oz. packages frozen broccoli
3 cups milk
5 eggs lightly beaten
1 tsp. salt
1 tsp. nutmeg
3 cups grated cheddar cheese

Thaw the broccoli and drain excess water. Heat milk by bringing it to a boil, then cool it to lukewarm. Mix eggs with salt and nutmeg and add milk and cheese, beating constantly. Pour into a greased 12" Dutch oven. Add broccoli. Bake 30-40 minutes, or until knife inserted comes out clean. Serves about 12 to 15.

Author's Note: Temperature was not listed in the letter. Try 250 degrees. You can also use the same recipe with cauliflower. Both make good side dishes. Cook until tender. If out camping, use most of heat on top for baking. 12 to 15 briquettes on top and 4 to 6 on the bottom. Don't get it too hot. Slow and easy is always best.

From Jody Markiewicz, Kerchikan, Alaska

Dutch Oven Chicken and Vegetables Casserole

½ lb. chicken per person
½ lb. vegetables per person—
    equal parts: potatoes, carrots, and celery (all cut up)
2 onions—chopped
1 bell pepper—chopped
2 or 3 cans cream of mushroom soup
2 or 3 cans cheddar cheese soup
seasoning to taste
14" Dutch oven

Brown the chicken. Add the vegetable mixture, then add the 2 onions and bell pepper. Mix together the cans of cream of mushroom soup and cheddar cheese soup and pour over the chicken and vegetables. Season to taste.

Cook until tender to the fork.

Author's Note: No temperature or time were listed so I use 250 degrees for 1½ hours. It will take longer or shorter, depending on how much you are cooking. Also, if you like your casseroles with more liquid, use 3 cans of each soup. If you like yours not so liquid, use only 2 of each soup.

Steve and Leanne also suggest that for a variation, instead of chicken use cubed turkey meat. Both are good. I will give you another idea. Use with a good roast or steak and that is very good, too.

From Steve and Leanne Stuart, North Ogden, Utah

Dutch Oven Mexican Roast Beef

2 lbs. round beef steak 2″ thick
3 tomatoes—cubed
3 tbsp. bacon grease
1 cup flour
1 clove garlic—chopped
2 onions—thick slices
1 tbsp. salt
1 tbsp. black pepper
2½ cups hot water
3 green chilies cut in half length-wise

Pound steak in flour and season. Heat grease in the Dutch oven. When hot, brown the steak on both sides. Add other ingredients. Cover and cook in oven until tender—about 1½ hours.

Author's Note: Temperature for cooking and the size of the oven were not in the recipe, nor was how many it will feed. Try a 12″ oven. That will hold most 2″-thick round steaks. Cook at about 250 degrees until tender to the fork. Will serve 5-6 people. If you don't like it hot with the chili peppers, use green peppers, or if you like it hotter, use hot peppers plus a dash of tabasco sauce.

From Richard O'Brien, Phoenix, Arizona

Chapter Eight

Dutch Oven Meat Dishes

In *Let's Cook Dutch,* on page 52, there is a recipe for hamburger steak with mushroom and onion. Since then I have found other ways to cook them in a Dutch oven. They are all good. I hope you want to try them. Select your favorite and see what can be done with plain ground beef.

The new recipes will be:
- Improved Dutch oven ground round steak with bacon, onions and mushrooms
- Dutch oven stuffed ground round steak
- Dutch oven breaded ground round steak

With these other recipes and the one in the first book, you can combine all the ideas, or vary them and try them the way you think will be best. Combining them will give you a lot of different ways to fix an easy good meat dish. It might surprise you how good they all are.

I start all of these recipes out cooking on top of the stove, but you can sure cook them outside over the hot coals or briquettes, as I have many times.

Improved Dutch Oven Ground Round Steak

1 lb. ground round (½ lb. per person) in patties
1 lg. sweet onion—chopped
4 oz. fresh mushrooms—sliced
¼ lb. bacon—cut in bite-size pieces
seasoning

This will make 2 steaks. If you need more, add 1 more onion for each 2 steaks and 4 oz. mushrooms for each. 2 more steaks ground round will be ½ lb. per person.

Now, put the oven over the right-sized burner. Start on medium high. Put in bacon, cook until brown. Add chopped onion, sliced mushrooms and season to taste. Brown on both sides. Turn over and put the mushroom, onion and bacon mixture on top of the steaks so they won't overcook. Cook until steaks are the way you like them.

I like these and the other ways, too. Whoever thought ground beef would be so good.

Breaded Ground Round Steak

½ lb. ground round per person, in patties
1 egg per steak
½ cup bread crumbs
½ cup cracker crumbs
1 lg. onion—chopped
¼ lb. bacon—cut in pieces
4 oz. sliced mushrooms
seasoning

On the stovetop put the size Dutch oven you will be cooking in on the right-sized burner. Set on medium high. Put in the bacon, onion and sliced mushrooms.

While cooking them until brown, put eggs in a pan large enough for the ground steaks to be dipped in. Mix up eggs and season to taste. Also, mix bread and cracker crumbs in a pan big enough to dip the steaks in.

Now, mold the ground meat into patties. Then dip them in the egg mixture and cover all over with the mixture, then remove. I use a spatula. Then put them in the breading mix. Set aside until the bacon, onions and mushrooms are browned. Then brown the steaks on both sides. Here you can leave them on top of the stove until they're done the way you like them, or pop them into the oven at 250 degrees until done. It will take about 15 minutes for medium well done. If you bake them, I like to mix 1 can of cream of mushroom soup and ½ can milk. Pour over the steaks when you put them in the oven. It surely makes a good steak.

When camping, it will be the same for all the recipes except don't put too much heat on the bottom. Cook slow and easy so they don't burn or dry out. Never press down on the patties. That forces out all the juice and they will be dry.

I hope by now you are hungry and ready to try one of these new ways for ground beef steaks. Enjoy them. I always do.

Stuffed Ground Round Steaks

¾ lb. ground round per person
3 tbsp. bacon grease or vegetable oil
seasoning
1 can cream of mushroom soup for every 2 steaks
½ can milk mixed in for every 2 steaks
¼ cup dressing or grated cheese per steak

Optional:
4 oz. sliced mushrooms for every 2 steaks
cream of chicken soup ⎱ in place of cream of
golden mushroom soup ⎰ mushroom

Take the ¾ lb. ground round and make 2 equal thin patties. Season to taste. Then, with the Dutch oven over the right-sized burner, get bacon grease or oil hot. Set on medium high, then brown patties on one side. When brown, turn them over and place stuffing in the middle. Then turn the other patty over it and carefully crimp the edges together with your finger and a spatula so you won't get burned. Now brown the patties on their other sides (both of them). Turn heat down to medium.

Pour the soup and milk mixed together over the steaks and cook until they're the way you like them. Watch them. It will only take about 15 minutes to cook medium well. If you want to cook mushrooms with them as I always do, brown them when you first brown the patties and keep over to the side. It will give extra flavor.

Also, if you would rather, you can bake them in the oven after all the patties are stuffed and browned and you pour the soup mix on them. Pop in the oven at 250 degrees for 10-15 minutes. I think this is my favorite way for ground round steak. I use cheese sometimes and dressing sometimes, but they are very good any way. If you don't have a good dressing mix, use the recipe in the complementary side dish section, or a package of store-bought dressing will do fine. As for the cheese, use the kind you like best. I have tried several and they all work well and taste good.

In the first of this section, I told you briefly about mixing up the recipes for all the ground meat steaks. I would like to explain more now about what I meant.

After reading all the different recipes, try them and then you can cook mushrooms, onions, and bacon for any of them. You can also stuff them and bake or fry them on top of the stove. Also, mix chopped onion right into the ground meat. Any of the combinations you want to try, I am sure will be good as I have tried them in every way and combination there is. I've never had a bad one. So try for yourself and surprise someone with a special ground round steak dinner.

I have made mention of ground round, but you can use any grade of ground beef. I use ground round because it has a lot less fat. If you do use regular ground beef always spoon out the excess grease before adding the cream soup and milk mixture. That way they will not be so greasy.

Dutch Oven Beef Roladen

thin sliced round steak
⅓ cup bacon grease or vegetable oil
1 tbsp. black pepper
a Stove Top Dressing
garlic salt
season salt
shredded cheese
finely chopped onion

Optional: Sliced dill pickle or sliced carrot stick

Before we get into the actual makings of Roladen, I want to give you a few hints that may help you.

First, ask your butcher to cut the round steak very thin for you, about ¼ " to ⅜ " thickness. Figure approximately ½ lb. per person as the least amount you want to fix. We have never had any left over when we have made it. Also, if round steak isn't available, use whatever good meat you can have sliced thin, with large enough slices to hold dressing and pickle when rolled. Next, you can use your own dressing or one of the store packaged ones.

We utilize the recipe we use for stuffing turkeys when at home, but when we are out camping we carry along a box of the packaged kind.

Last, the mixture you layer on the beef to roll up can be anything you choose. I use jack, mozzarella, and cheddar cheeses. Use the one you and your family like best. Or use a combination of two as I do. Don't be afraid to try variations of things you like.

Now you take the slices of steak and lay them flat on the cutting board. Season to taste. If the slices are too large, cut them down so that you can roll them and hold them together with two toothpicks. Larger than this is too hard to handle. Now on each piece of meat place a small amount of dressing, sprinkle with finely chopped onion, and add a slice of cheese and a slice of dill pickle or carrot stick. Roll up the slices of meat, tucking in the ends and securing the roll with two toothpicks. They are now ready to be cooked.

Put oil in the Dutch oven and place it over the nearest-to-size burner on your stove if cooking indoors. Turn heat to medium high and when grease is hot, put all of the Roladen into the grease. Brown on both sides. Use tongs to turn the meat, so as not to puncture it. When brown all around, turn the heat down to low. Cover and cook until tender. Use the juice to make a tasty gravy.

If you want, after browning the Roladen, you can turn your oven on to 250° and finish cooking this way until they are tender. Cook about 30 to 40 minutes, depending on the thickness of the meat and how many you are cooking. Just keep an eye on them. They are certainly worth the little bit of extra work they take.

Serve with a baked potato and your favorite vegetable. You can bake the potato while waiting for the Roladen to get done.

If cooking them outside, remember to take some of the briquettes or coals out from under the Dutch oven after you have browned the meat and put them on top of the lid. You want them to cook slowly and not burn on the bottom.

Dutch Oven Stuffed Flank Steak

1 - 2 lb. flank steak
seasoning
¼ cup bacon grease or vegetable oil or margarine
1 can golden mushroom soup
1 cup milk
¼ cup celery—chopped
¼ cup onions—chopped
1 cup corn bread stuffing or
    special stuffing of your choice

The flank steak is a special-flavored cut of meat. As I said on pages 40-41 of *Let's Cook Dutch,* I use it a lot now. Here is another way to fix it. I think you will like it when you try it. When you select the flank steak, get one that weighs about 2 lbs. That will give you ½ lb. per person. The above recipe will serve 4, so if you need more, you will know about what to get for the number of people for whom you are cooking.

Now trim the steak of extra fat or gristle, then season to taste. Put the Dutch oven on top of the stove on medium high, or heat it if out camping. When hot, put in bacon grease, vegetable oil or margarine (whatever you are using). Add chopped celery and onion. While they are cooking, tenderize the steak with a meat mallet—not too hard but a little—then put the meat into the Dutch oven and sear it on both sides. That will keep the juice in. Then remove the steak. Add water and boil it, then stir in the stuffing mixture. Remove from the heat. Score one side of the flank steak with diamond cuts. Turn that side down and spoon in the stuffing mixture to which you have added the celery and onions. Roll it up like a jelly roll. Skewer the steak, then brown it on all sides. While it is browning, mix the can of golden mushroom soup with the cup of milk in a separate bowl. When the steak is brown, turn off the heat on top of the stove and pour the soup mixture over the meat. Season to taste.

Put into the oven at 250 degrees with the lid on until tender (about 1½ to 2 hours depending on how much you are cooking, maybe even longer). Just watch it and when it's tender, remove from the Dutch oven. Cut in pieces. Spoon the gravy over it. Serve with a side dish you like, maybe potatoes and salad with rolls or the hot french bread I told you about in this book. That is good eating! A good vegetable goes well, too.

For a variation, you can use round steak but tenderize it well first. This flank steak stuffed is worth the effort to fix. Try it.

Dutch Oven Stuffed Meat Loaf

   2 lbs. ground round beef
   2 eggs
   2 tbsp. dry onion
   seasoning

   2-3 cups dressing/stuffing
   1 can cream of mushroom soup
   1 can golden cream of mushroom soup
   1 cup milk

On pages 45 and 46 of *Let's Cook Dutch* I gave you a recipe for meat loaf. If you tried it you know it was good. But now I have another way for you to try it.

Keep dressing/stuffing, soups and 1 cup milk aside.

Combine all the other ingredients. Season to taste and form into a loaf. It if's too big to handle, form two loaves. Now, in the center of the loaf, push down and out with your hands to make a pocket. Then fill the pocket with some dressing and form the meat over to close up the pocket.

Now it's ready for the gravy. Mix up the soups with 1 cup of milk. Put the meat loaves in the Dutch oven. Pour the gravy mix over the loaves. Put in the oven on 250 degrees for about 1 hour. Watch it so it does not go dry. When it is done, serve with the gravy on the side. I want to tell you that is some kind of good!

Now, if you're out camping, remember to put most of the heat on top of the Dutch oven. Use only about 4-6 briquettes on the bottom, but 15-18 on the top. It will still cook in about 1 hour.

If by any chance there is any left over, keep it for lunch the next day. Slice the meat loaf and put the dressing on the side. Serve with your favorite vegetable. Pour gravy over the meat and dressing. Hot rolls or biscuits go well with it, too. Then you can sop up all the gravy. Leftovers can be good after all!

Dutch Oven Brisket with Vegetables

1 2-2½ lb. fresh brisket (thin end)
6 medium potatoes cut in 8 pieces each
6 medium carrots—sliced
3 medium onions—sliced
seasoning
dash paprika
1 bay leaf
2 tbsp. bacon grease, butter or margarine
3 tbsp. all purpose flour
1 tsp. beef flavor gravy base
1½ cups water

First trim the excess fat from the brisket, then pound it with a semi-sharp knife. This will break up the meat fibers and will make it more tender. A meat tenderizer mallet will work, too. Season the brisket to taste. Add a dash of paprika and the bay leaf. Now brown the brisket on both sides using the bacon grease, butter or margarine on top of the stove set on medium high. When browned, add 1½ cups water and the potatoes, onion, and carrots. Season to taste. Put into the oven now, set on 200 or 225 degrees, and cook until tender.

This is a good meal, but it must be cooked on low heat for a longer time. When the meat is as tender as you want it, remove it with the vegetables from the Dutch oven. Take the bay leaf out, too.

Now prepare the gravy. Add water if needed (½ cup) and slowly, on top of the stove, add the 1 tsp. beef flavor gravy base and stir in the 3 tbsp. flour to thicken it. Don't get it too hot. Medium will be plenty now.

Cut the brisket into serving pieces. Put it in a bowl with the vegetables. Pour gravy over it all and you have a good tasty meal with rolls or oven-hot french bread. You also can use a flank steak for this recipe or a brisket for the stuffed flank steak recipe.

One last thing: always cut the meat across the grain. That's a lot more tender for any meat. Will serve 6. If you need more, adjust the recipe to meet your need.

If you want to cook this dish out camping, do it all the same, just keep the heat low and do it when it can cook a while.

Also, if wanted you can use whatever vegetables you like. These are the three main ones I use, but corn and cauliflower go well, too. Try it and see what you like best.

Dutch Oven Pot Roast with Sour Cream and Mushroom Gravy

½ lb. roast beef per person
3 tsp. bacon grease or vegetable oil
1 beef bouillon cube
1 cup boiling water
4 tsp. catsup
1 tsp. Worcestershire sauce
1 small onion—chopped
½ clove garlic—minced
2 tsp. salt
½ tsp. pepper
1 tsp. celery salt
1 small can mushrooms
4 tsp. flour
1 cup sour cream

In a Dutch oven on top of the stove, put bacon grease or vegetable oil. Brown the roast on all sides. Dissolve the bouillon cube in the one cup boiling water. Add to roast. Add catsup, Worcestershire sauce, chopped onion, salt, garlic, celery salt, and pepper. Stir it up. Put the lid on and cook in the oven at 250 degrees for 2 to 2½ hours, until the meat is tender. Remove from oven. Take meat from the Dutch oven. Blend flour into the liquid to make gravy. Add mushrooms and stir in the sour cream. Slice the beef and serve with the gravy over it. Good eating!

If out camping, do it the same way. Just don't let the fire get too hot. Also, if cooking a big roast for a lot of people, you will need to increase the ingredients to cover the extra people. Judge for yourself what amount you will need.

Cook some extra if you have big eaters. They will all want second helpings.

Navajo Taco

Bean and Meat Topping

    ¼ cup oil
    2 large onions—chopped
    2 cloves garlic or 2 tsp. garlic powder
Saute' in Dutch oven. When tender add:
    6-8 tsp. chili powder
    2 lbs. ground beef
    3 tsp. salt
When meat is brown, drain grease and add:
    2 cans pinto beans
    1 15 oz. can tomato sauce
Heat 10 minutes.

This topping is put on top of fry bread and then topped with your choice of the following:

Lettuce, cheese, onions, tomato, bell pepper, etc.

You will find this a delicious alternative to the standard taco.

Dutch Oven Fry Bread

4¼ cups flour
1 tbsp. baking powder
1 tbsp. salt
1 tbsp. powdered milk
1½ cups warm water
1½ cups oil or shortening (to fry the bread)

Sift the dry ingredients together. Add warm water, mix, knead dough for a few minutes until smooth. Let sit 1 hour.

Take pieces of dough and stretch or roll flat, then brown in hot oil until golden brown.

These can be used for pizza crusts or as a base for Navajo Tacos. They are also very good plain with butter and honey.

Dutch Oven Lamb Stew

2 cups water
2 lbs. lamb cut in pieces
2 tbsp. flour
2 tbsp. bacon grease or vegetable oil
3 cups carrots—chopped
6 medium potatoes cut in 8ths
2 cups onion—chopped
1-2 cups celery—chopped
salt and pepper to taste
1 can tomatoes (optional)

For top of the stove, put the Dutch oven over the right-sized burner. Turn to medium high. Put in the bacon grease or vegetable oil. Put the cut up lamb into a pan. Roll it in flour and season to taste, then put it into the Dutch oven and brown it all over. Then turn heat down to medium low. Add water and let it simmer for 30 to 40 minutes while you prepare the vegetables. Put in the carrots first, they take longer to cook. Then the other veggies. Cook until tender, about 30 to 45 minutes. Serves about 6 to 8 depending on the size of the servings.

Options:

You can cover the stew with biscuits (about 10-15) before it is done and cook until the biscuits are brown and vegetables are also, and you have lamb stew pie.

If you like stew with tomato flavor, add 1 large can of tomatoes. When you have the vegetables almost done, mix it in for flavor. No matter how you like it, this is a good way to cook lamb.

Dutch Oven Bar-B-Q Meat Stew

> 3 lbs. pork loin roast
> 3 lbs. beef roast
> 3 lbs. chicken
> ¼ cup liquid smoke
> 1 qt. bottle hickory smoke Bar-B-Q sauce
> ⅓ cup bacon grease or vegetable oil
> seasoning

On top of the stove put the Dutch oven. Add the bacon grease or vegetable oil. While it is getting hot, season the meat to taste and put into the Dutch oven. Brown it all, then put into the oven at 300 degrees. Cook until the meat is tender (about 2½ hours). Remove from the oven. Cut all the meat into small pieces. Take out all the bones. Put meat back into the Dutch oven. Add liquid smoke and hickory smoke Bar-B-Q sauce. If not enough broth, mix 1 chicken or beef bouillon cube in a cup of hot water and add to the broth. Mix it in. Put the lid on the Dutch oven and put it back into the oven. Turn heat down to 200 degrees. Cook about 1 hour.

Will serve 8 to 10 people. Use over rice with vegetable of your choice and corn bread or hot rolls. It will be a special meal. I like it with Dutch oven potatoes or the Dutch oven potato cakes recipe in the Miscellaneous Goodies Section.

Chapter Nine

Tri Tip Dutch Oven Recipes

Introduction

In this section I will tell you about a special cut of meat called Tri Tip and some of the ways I use it in Dutch oven cooking. Because of its flavor, I prefer it to any other cut of beef. It is never tough and always cooks up just like I want it to. For that reason, I want to share the Tri Tip with all of you that read this book so you can enjoy it, too.

The Tri Tip is the butt end of the sirloin and will weigh from ½ pound up to about 4 pounds. The grain of the meat can go in 3 directions, which is where the name Tri Tip comes from.

Look at the Tri Tip closely. Pick out a large one. If you are going to cut the steaks out of the center, you can only get from 1 to 3, but they are worth the effort. See the accompanying pictures on how to cut them and what to do with the two outer sides of the Tri Tip when you have cut the steaks. Here's what to do with the steaks you cut out of the center of the Tri Tip.

Using a sharp slicing knife, cut the Tri Tip across the grain at the widest part and come in from the edge so you can get as long a cut as possible. Then cut the steak about ¾ of an inch thick. Cut one or two more if you can, but don't get too close to the edge. You should have a thin piece of meat left on both sides when you finish.

For every Tri Tip you cut steaks from, you will have 2 small pieces of meat and 1 to 3 steaks. I always buy 1 case of Tri Tip at a time (that is 4 bags, with 6 Tri Tips to a bag average), and the bags will weigh from 15 to 18 pounds each. The total for a case should be 72 pounds or more. That way you will have larger Tri Tips. I get them this way so I will have a good selection and can cut steaks from most of them. But you can buy smaller amounts.

I freeze the steaks in packages of 2 with the fat on so I can cook them as regular steaks, or take the fat off and pound them with a meat hammer for chicken-fried steaks, swiss steak, stroganoff or phillys.

The pieces of Tri Tip which are left after the steaks are cut from it are frozen in packages of 3 or 4—that will be about the right size for pot roast phillys or whatever.

Not all of the Tri Tip in each bag will be large enough or right for steaks. We always like to freeze these and mark them "whole Tri Tip" for that time when we want to fix a special roast.

The Tri Tip is a special cut and not available everywhere. It you can't find it in your area, use a sirloin tip roast, sirloin steaks, or eye of round roast and cut it into steaks. It will be good, but not quite like Tri Tip. But you have to make do sometimes with what is handy. I have used sirloin too, and round steak. They were not as tender so I had to cook them longer, but they were still very good. I have taken a piece of the eye of the round, sliced it into steaks for chicken-fried steaks and swiss steak. It was good also and made very good stroganoff.

1. Select the better and larger tri tips to cut into steaks.

2. Then cut off the end of the tri tip. Make sure to cut across the grain so you can get full-size steaks ½ to ¾ inch thick.

3. Cut two or three steaks from the center of the tri tip.

4. With each tri tip you cut there will be two or three steaks and the two outside ends to use in other tri tip recipes.

5. If you're going to use the cut steaks for chicken-fried or Swiss steak, cut off the strip of fat. Here you see tri tip steaks cut for chicken-fried steaks with the fat strip cut off and ready to be pounded with a meat hammer.

Tri Tip Roast

As I said in the chapter introduction, not all tri tip can be cut into steaks. We like them whole for pot roast. The leftover pieces, after the steaks are cut, can also be used for roast or you can cut them in small pieces for phillys. I freeze them to use when needed. We will go over the steak recipes on succeeding pages.

Now if using a full tri tip, this is how I do it. Because I love mushrooms, I cook them with it.

1 tri tip roast
2 oz. sliced mushrooms per person
1 tbsp. bacon grease or vegetable oil
seasoning
1 potato per person, cut in quarters
1 onion per person, cut in quarters
4-6 baby carrots per person, or carrots cut in quarters

As you will know your eating habits, cook the amount needed to feed the number of people present. Two or three slices of roast per person with the vegetables should be enough. When you cook the leftover pieces which resulted from cutting the steaks, allow one piece of meat per person. Don't worry if you have cooked extra as you will most likely want a second helping.

Now to start with, on the top of the stove put the Dutch oven over the right-sized burner. Put in the bacon grease or vegetable oil. While it's getting hot, season the meat and brown it on all sides. Add the mushrooms and brown them, too. When the meat is brown, put it fat-side down, and put your Dutch oven into the oven with the lid on. Set at 250 degrees, cook for 1 hour, then add the vegetables as listed above to top off the tri tip. After about 1 more hour, when the meat is tender and all the vegetables are done, take the vegetables out, except for the mushrooms, and put them into a bowl to keep warm while you remove the meat. Cut off the fat and slice it, then put it back in the juice with the mushrooms. Let simmer a couple minutes while you get everything ready. Then serve the meat, mushrooms with juice and the vegetables. I like the juice over the meat and the vegetables—this has always been a special dish.

A few more hints: If you cook a lot of meat and can't get it into one layer, put the top layer with the fat-side up. If too crowded, use a larger-size Dutch oven. You will need room for the vegetables.

When you check the meat, if it is getting dry, make up some juice as needed by adding 1 beef bouillon cube to a cup of warm water. This will help cook the meat and the juice will have a good flavor. If necessary you can add 1 additional cup of warm water, in case there is no bouillon around the meat, and the Dutch oven will give it flavor. So try it and enjoy.

Introduction to Tri Tip Dutch Oven Steaks

Before we get into the recipes, I want to tell you why I have a section in this book just for the tri tip and the steaks that are cut from it. It is a very special-flavored piece of meat. Even though I also like New York, T-Bone and Fillets, the steaks cut from the tri tip roast are still the ones I eat most often. All of the steaks have always been very good and that is why there are pictures and directions on how to cut them. So now I will tell you how to cook them so that you can also see for yourself how good they are.

One last tip: if you cut the steaks to serve as steak with mushrooms and onions or as baked steak, leave the strip of fat on. If you cut them to serve as Swiss steak, chicken-fried steak or stroganoff, cut the fat off so it won't be in the way when you tenderize with the meat hammer.

Tri Tip Steak with Mushrooms and Onions

2 pieces bacon per person, cut in pieces
1 steak per person
¼ cup sliced mushrooms per person
¼ cup diced onions per person
seasoning

On top of the stove, put your Dutch oven over the right-sized burner, turn to medium high. Put in the bacon and when brown add the mushrooms and onions. Cook until they are brown, then season the steaks to taste and brown them on both sides. Turn with tongs or spatula. (Don't stick the steaks with a fork—the juice will come out.) Now turn the heat down to medium low. Cook until tender to the fork or however you like to eat your steak. Spoon the mushrooms and onions out of the Dutch oven over each steak and be ready for a treat.

Tri Tip Baked Steak

Before I tell you about how to cook them, you might like to know how I discovered another way to cook steak in a Dutch oven.

I love to fish. One time when we were up at our summer place, we came back late and ready to eat. Not wanting to wait 30-40 minutes for a fire to be ready to Bar-B-Q the steaks we had defrosted, I got out a Dutch oven to cook them inside, where it was light and warm. They came out so good that now I always plan to fix them this way. So if you want steak quick, try it sometime.

Now for the recipe.

    1 steak per person
    1 tbsp. bacon grease or vegetable oil
    1 can cream of mushroom soup
    ½ can milk
    seasoning

On top of the stove, put your Dutch oven over the right-sized burner on medium high. Put in the bacon grease or vegetable oil. While it's getting hot, season steaks to taste. Brown on both sides. Then pour in the mushroom soup and the milk. Mix it all up. Turn the heat off on top and pop the Dutch oven, with the lid on, into the oven at 300 degrees for about 15-20 minutes, or until the steaks are as you like them.

I like to add any leftover potatoes to one side of the Dutch oven when you put the steaks into the stove oven so that when the steaks are ready, the potatoes will be, too. That way you can have a complete meal in 30 minutes or less, by also cooking a frozen vegetable in a pan on the stove and making rolls or bread. Use the mushroom soup over the meat and potatoes—it's good eating for a starving fisherman.

Tri Tip Stroganoff with Noodles

With the steaks cut out of the center of the tri tip, or with ones too small to cut steaks from, you can cut into small pieces and make one of my favorite recipes: Stroganoff.

> 4 oz. tri tip meat in strips, per person
> ½ cup sour cream
> 1 cup milk
> 2-3 tbsp. bacon grease or oil
> mushrooms—sliced
>
> *Optional:* home-made noodles

Cut the tri tip in slices across the grain. Trim off the fat and gristle, if any. In your Dutch oven put the bacon grease or vegetable oil and, when hot, season the meat strips and place in the hot oil to brown. Add the sliced mushrooms to brown also. Turn over with a spatula or tongs. While the meat is browning, in a separate bowl mix the ½ cup sour cream, 1 cup milk and seasoning to taste. After the meat and the mushrooms are brown, add the sour cream mixture to them, mixing well with the juice of the meat.

Let it simmer on low heat until tender. Then dip it out of the Dutch oven over the noodles. One can almost smell and taste it just thinking about it.

Home-Made Noodles for Stroganoff, Soup, Etc.

> 7 eggs
> 1 tsp. salt
> ½ cup milk
> 5 cups flour
>
> ⅓ cup vegetable oil

Put the eggs, salt, milk and flour in a bowl and mix well until thick and consistent. Roll thin on a flour base board and cut into thin strips. Drop into boiling water that you have put the butter or vegetable oil into and let cook until tender. They will float when they are ready to put on the plate for stroganoff or into the soup to be discussed in the soup section.

Dutch Oven Chicken-Fried Steaks

For a special treat, how about Dutch Oven Chicken-Fried Steaks?

    1 tri tip steak per person
    1 cup cracker meal
    1 cup bread crumbs
    ½ cup milk
    ½ cup buttermilk
    seasoning
    1 egg
    2″ of vegetable oil in the Dutch oven
    (can be strained and used again)

In one bowl mix ½ cup bread crumbs and ½ cup cracker meal.

In another bowl mix 1 egg, ½ cup buttermilk, ½ cup milk, and season to taste. Then take the steaks and pound them flat with a meat-tenderizing hammer. When flat, dip them in the batter and then in the bowl with the cracker meal and bread crumbs. Sprinkle over the steak and push into the meat. Turn over and do it on the other side, too. The steak will be double in size. If you like a lot of batter and coating you can double dip them but they will be big. I only dip mine once. They will be the size of a large plate then.

Now when the chicken-fried steaks are about ready, put enough oil in the Dutch oven. You will need it to be about 2″ deep. When the oil is hot put the steaks in. Cook until brown and turn over. When brown and floating they will be ready to eat. Take out of the oven. Put on paper towels to remove the excess oil, then on the plate. I think these are the best chicken-fried steaks you will ever have.

A couple of pointers: don't pound the steak too thin or it will fall apart when putting into the batter or pushing it into the bread crumbs and cracker meal. If it does fall apart, cook as separate steaks. They will be fine for kids or anyone that can't eat a whole one.

The 1 cup bread crumbs, 1 cup cracker meal, ½ cup buttermilk, ½ cup milk and 1 egg will be enough for about 2 or 3 steaks. So if you're going to cook more, then add what you need. The breading can be strained and used again.

Swiss Steak with Baby Carrots

The tri tip cut into slices makes good Swiss steak, too. Try it also.

8 oz. thick sliced tri tip, per person
2 onions—sliced
1 cup mushrooms—sliced
1 cup baby carrots—fresh or frozen
¼ cup bacon grease or vegetable oil
seasoning
flour

Optional:
1 can cream of mushroom soup
½ can milk

Put the bacon grease or vegetable oil into your Dutch oven. While it's getting hot, take the pieces of cut-up meat and bread them with the flour so they are coated. Season to taste and when the oven is hot, put in the sliced onions and sliced mushrooms, then the meat. Brown the meat on both sides together with the onions and mushrooms. When all are brown, add the baby carrots. Lower the heat so that all will cook slowly until the meat and carrots are tender. It is a special dish.

As a special option you can add a mushroom sauce. Just use 1 can of cream of mushroom soup and ½ can milk, mix together and pour over the steak. You can also make a gravy out of the juice left in the Dutch oven. Try both, or your own idea. It will be very good whichever way you try it.

Dutch Oven Philly

One of my favorite sandwiches is a Dutch Oven Philly. Use a small tri tip cut into small pieces across the grain.

8 oz. tri tip cut in small strips
8 oz. mushrooms—diced
8 oz. onions—diced
⅓ cup bacon grease or vegetable oil
Optional: slice of cheese for each sandwich

To your Dutch oven add the bacon grease. When hot, add the onions and mushrooms. Let them brown a little, then add the strips of meat. Mix well and let simmer on low heat with lid on the oven until tender (about ½ hour—less if only doing a little). Put on good french rolls. You can even brown these first if you want. It makes a special sandwich. If any is left over, leave it in a sandwich-size serving. Put it in a sandwich bag and freeze it for another time. Warm it in the microwave and it will be like fresh made. I don't do that very often—there are never any left.

Now as an option, try a slice of jack, Swiss or cheddar cheese on them. If you like cheese, add it when the meat is first put on the bun and it will melt into the meat. If you cut the cheese too thick, pop it into the Dutch oven for a minute until the cheese melts.

It works well too, to put them in sandwich-size servings in the Dutch oven. Put the sliced cheese on each. Replace the lid and let it cook low for a minute or so. When the cheese melts, they are ready to put onto a roll or bread and eat. It will be a special sandwich for you, too.

This will make 3 or 4 sandwiches. If you want to make more, cook equal amounts of the meat, mushroom and onions. For a big sandwich on a french roll, figure 8 oz. for each person. As it will cook down, always cook extra. For some reason, around our house they all get eaten. Even our grandkids like them so they must be special.

Chapter Ten

Poultry and Fish

Dutch Oven Stuffed Game Hens

> 1 game hen per person
> enough wild rice or dressing to stuff them
> 2 tbsp. bacon grease or vegetable oil
> seasoning

I enjoy game hens, and I think they taste better cooked in a Dutch oven than any other way. All you Dutch oven chefs, I'm sure, will agree. So next time they go on sale or you just feel like having some, try them this way.

First, stuff the hens with wild rice or dressing. Then sew them up. On top of the stove, on medium high, put them in the hot bacon grease or vegetable oil in your Dutch oven. Season to taste. Brown the hens on all sides, then add ½ cup water. Put the lid on the Dutch oven and pop in the oven at 250 degrees for about 45 minutes or until tender to the fork.

A better-tasting bird will be hard to find.

I like to make a gravy out of the drippings. Remove the birds. Put the Dutch oven on top of the stove. When the juice is simmering add flour and mix it in until smooth. Season to taste, and pour over each bird. Serve while warm. If you don't have enough juice for gravy you can add a cup of chicken bouillon to what you have and thicken as above. Also, you can make a gravy out of cream of chicken soup. This is good. Or, try 1 can soup and ½ can milk. Mix together and pour over the hens.

Just before you take them out, spoon gravy on each bird. A 12″ Dutch oven will cook 5-6 birds, depending on how fat they are. The cream of chicken soup will be enough for that many. If you need to cook more, use a 14″ oven, 2 cans cream of chicken soup and 1 can of milk. Work at it. You will find the right amount of gravy to fix as you will know the eating habits of those present.

If fixing them while out camping, prepare them about the same. Just don't get them too hot, or try to cook them too fast. They can easily dry out.

Hope you like them as much as we do.

Dutch Oven Rabbit

2-3 rabbit pieces per person
3 tbsp. bacon grease or vegetable oil
buttermilk—enough to soak the rabbit in
flour—enough for breading
    or bread and cracker crumbs for breading

If the rabbit is home raised or store bought, cut in pieces and soak in buttermilk at least 1 hour. If cooking wild rabbits, soak them in buttermilk at least 4 hours. While they are soaking, keep them in a cold place—in the refrigerator at home or in an ice chest when out camping. You don't want them to spoil before you can cook them. Now for the recipe.

For top of the stove, put your Dutch oven on the right-sized burner. Set heat at medium high. If out camping, get the Dutch oven ready, and then put in the grease or vegetable oil. While it is getting hot, take the rabbits out of the buttermilk and put them in the breading mix or flour. Season to taste and brown in the hot Dutch oven. Move pieces around until all are brown. Put the Dutch oven (with lid on) into your stove oven. Cook at 250-300 degrees until tender—about 1 hour.

If out camping, take most of the heat from the bottom and place on the lid for baking. The rabbits will still cook in about an hour.

I like Dutch oven rabbit as much as Dutch oven chicken. I don't really like chicken except when cooked in a Dutch oven. Rabbits are very good this way. For those of you that have never tried rabbit, you should try it this way. You are missing a treat.

Remember to save the left-over juice and rabbit for the next recipe in this section.

Dutch Oven Rabbit Pot Pie

1 cup bite size pieces of boneless rabbit, per person
1 cup onions—chopped
1 cup carrots—chopped
1 cup celery—chopped
1 cup potatoes—chopped
3 cups combined leftover juice (from *Dutch Oven Rabbit*)
    and water, or 1 cup chicken bouillon and 2 cups water
seasoning

3¼ cups biscuit mix
1 cup milk

12" Dutch oven for 5-6 people, or 14" Dutch oven
    for 7 or more

Put the Dutch oven on top of the stove over the right-sized burner, or on briquettes if out camping. Add the juice or bouillon and water, up to 3 cups. Put in all the chopped-up vegetables. Season to taste. Put the lid on the oven and cook on medium high. After 15 minutes or so, they should be about done. Add the cut-up boneless rabbit. Turn down to medium to simmer while you mix up the top crust.

Combine 3¼ cups biscuit mix with 1 cup milk. Mix until dough forms. Beat about 30 seconds. If the dough is too sticky, gradually mix in enough biscuit mix to make the dough easy to handle, but no more than ¼ cup. Then roll it out on a surface with more biscuit mix on it so it won't stick.

Knead the dough about 10 times. Roll out about a 12" circle to cover a 12" Dutch oven to the edges. Now take the lid off the Dutch oven and turn the heat off.

Stir the contents well. Add a little water and seasoning if needed, then put the rolled crust on top. Bake in the oven at 350 degrees for 8 to 10 minutes, until the crust is golden brown. If you leave the lid off it will bake faster. It sure makes a good meal!

You can also use the same recipe with chicken, beef or pork roast leftovers and their gravy or juice. A 12" pie will serve 4-6, depending on how much you eat. If you need more, increase the recipe and use a 14" Dutch oven.

I use 1 more cup of biscuit mix, ⅓ cup more milk and 2 cups of everything else to feed 8-10 if someone doesn't take too much.

Try it with left-over meat and juice or gravy. No one will know they are having leftovers.

The large rolled-out crust is harder to position than the biscuits. I think that is why I use biscuits—it's easy to cut them and set them on the top. Bake them also until golden brown—about 8 minutes. Any way it is good.

Dutch Oven Fish Fillets

1 fillet per person
eggs
lemon juice—optional
bread crumbs
cracker crumbs
seasoning
1 tbsp. vegetable oil or butter

For all you other fish lovers—this one's for you. In *Let's Cook Dutch,* on page 64, I gave you a good recipe for trout—the way I do them. This one is for any kind of fish fillets you like. My favorite, besides trout, are sole, catfish, orange roughy, and cod. Also, salmon and halibut. These are usually cut into steaks. With the breading on them it is harder to see bones but they are very good this way, too. So watch for the bones and try them all, or your favorite fish if not listed here.

In a pan big enough for the fish fillets to fit in, beat up the egg. In a separate pan, mix the bread and cracker crumbs. Season to taste, then dip fillets in the egg and then in crumbs. Do both sides. Now on top of the stove, put the Dutch oven on the right-sized burner on top of the stove and set temperature to medium. Put a tablespoon of butter or vegetable oil in the Dutch oven. When hot, brown the fish fillets on both sides; it only takes 2 or 3 minutes. Turn the heat down to low. Cook with the lid on the Dutch oven until tender. If desired, add a drop or two of lemon juice to each fillet. Serve with tarter sauce and your favorite side dish (Dutch oven potato always goes well with it).

A few tips to remember: if fillets are thick they will take a little longer to cook. If you like, just pop them into the oven at about 225 degrees until tender. Halibut and salmon steaks will take longer, but in the oven they come out very good. You will need 1 egg for approximately every 2 fillets. If you don't want to put seasoning into the crumb mixture, season to taste after dipping in the egg mixture and crumbs. I like butter for browning fish, but vegetable oil will work fine, too. Try your next fish fillets this way. Dutch ovens help them to taste better.

Mike's Dutch Oven Chicken with Special Oatmeal Dressing

This is a recipe that my son-in-law came up with and agreed to let me include in this book.

2-3 pieces chicken per person

Dressing:
3 cups oatmeal (whole, not instant)
2 eggs
1 tbsp. sage
1 tsp. onion salt
1 cup celery—chopped
1 large onion—chopped
½ tsp. salt
½ tsp. pepper
½ cup oil
1 cup milk or water
1 cup cornmeal

Mix all dressing ingredients together and place them in a mound in the center of your 14" Dutch oven.

Sprinkle the chicken with sage, salt and pepper and place around the dressing. Add 3 cups of water.

INDOORS
Cook in a regular oven, covered, for 2 hours at 350°.

OUTDOORS
Be sure the heat is mostly on top so the dressing doesn't burn. This should be checked every 30 minutes.

This recipe was a result of experimenting when there were no bread crumbs in the house. Try it and you will be surprised at how good it is.

Chapter Eleven

Dutch Oven Sandwiches

Dutch Oven Philly Burgers with Cheese

½ lb. ground round per person
3 medium onions
1 cup mushrooms (8 oz. pkg.)
½ lb. bacon
2 cups grated cheese
seasoning (salt and pepper)

Before I tell you how to make them, you might be interested in where the recipe came from and why. We were at a family reunion at Bear Lake. When out camping with a bunch that like to eat as we do, we always take too much food. After a few days the meat had to be used! So, not wanting to waste it, the time came to think up something besides cheese burgers. Therefore, philly burgers were born and were so good that from now on we will be making them.

Now the recipe:
Chop up the bacon in bite-size pieces. Also chop up the onions and mushrooms.

Cook the bacon until almost crisp, add the onions and mushrooms and cook until brown. Add the ground round and season to taste. Mix in with the bacon, onion and mushrooms. Cook until brown. When the meat is done, add the grated cheese. Stir it in until melted, then spoon out on rolls, bread, french bread or whatever you have.

We cooked the first batch on a camp stove with a 14″ Dutch oven over one burner, but they are so good, you can do it on your stove at home, on a camp stove, or with briquettes.

We like to toast the rolls or bread, too. Just put a little butter or margarine in a Dutch oven on medium high. When the butter melts, put the rolls in—it only takes a few minutes and they taste so good.

To clean up, wipe the Dutch oven with a paper towel and you are all set for the next time. Don't get the Dutch oven too hot or you might burn the butter, making it harder to clean.

Dutch Oven Sloppy Joes

When making Sloppy Joes it is important to know approximately how many you are planning on serving so that you will know the quantities needed. These amounts also depend on the size of the Sloppy Joes themselves.

One pound of lean ground beef (plus all the other ingredients) makes about eight regular-sized Sloppy Joes.

So put on your thinking cap, decide how many you want and adjust the amounts accordingly.

> 1 lb. lean ground beef
> ¼ lb. bacon (cut up)
> 1 medium-sized onion—chopped
> 1 cup hickory smoked Bar-B-Q sauce
> 1 tsp. all purpose seasoning

If cooking indoors, put the Dutch oven over the appropriate burner. Turn to medium high heat. When warm, place the bacon in it, stirring with a spatula after it has started cooking. Add the chopped onions and continue cooking until the bacon is done and the onions are light brown. Add the ground beef—seasoned to taste—and mix it with the onion/bacon mixture until the ground beef is brown. Turn the heat down to medium.

Now, this is very important. If there is a lot of grease in the mixture, spoon it off. Get as much out as you possibly can. You don't need or want a lot of grease in the Sloppy Joes. Then add the Bar-B-Q sauce. I like the hickory smoked one but if your preference is the plain variety, use your favorite brand or recipe.

Mix it all well and let simmer for about 10 minutes. Keep warm until you are ready to serve it on buns. I think you might be surprised at how good these are. I have made these for a lot of people and many have said they are the best they have ever tasted.

If you're cooking outside, just make sure your oven is not too hot. You don't need intense heat to cook ground meat. Then just follow the same directions, removing most of the heat when it comes to simmering the mixture.

Just an extra hint. Try placing a slice of cheese on top of the mixture after you spoon it on the bun. The heat from the meat will make it melt a little—it's absolutely delicious.

Enjoy!

Bar-B-Q Sandwich

If you have any meat left over, there is another good sandwich you might enjoy.

Cut the meat in small pieces. Let simmer in the Dutch oven in any left-over juice. Add Bar-B-Q sauce and let simmer until tender. If there is no juice from roast or steaks, just let the meat simmer in the Bar-B-Q sauce.

Put it on a good French roll or whatever you happen to have. You can use any meat you want or have left over. If no juice, make 1 cup by dissolving 1 beef bouillon cube in a cup of hot water. Season to taste, and after simmering, add the hickory smoked Bar-B-Q sauce. It will make a very tasty hot sandwich. If you like yours spicy, add 1 teaspoon tabasco sauce.

Patty Melt

½ lb. good ground round per person
1 tbsp. bacon grease or vegetable oil
rye bread
sliced cheese for each
sliced onion for each
seasoning
1 tbsp. butter or margarine

You can make this recipe several ways. I will describe how I do it and it might be just how you like it, too. Or you can create your own.

I sometimes chop up the onion and mix it with the ground beef—then form the patty. Put the bacon grease in the Dutch oven.

When hot put in the patties and cook on medium, browning on both sides.

Spoon out all the excess grease. On one side of your Dutch oven brown the rye bread, buttered side down.

Now you can add the cheese to the top of the burger patty so that it will melt. When the burger is the way you like it (well, medium or rare), and the cheese has melted, take the rye bread out and put the brown side down. Put the patty on top, and top it with another piece of bread. Cut in half so that it is easier to handle. Now, if you don't like rye bread, use buns, French bread or whatever you like. But you will be happy with the tasty burger no matter what type of bread it is on.

For those who don't like onions, you may choose to not mix them in or have a slice on top. As to the cheese—it is a matter of personal choice. I have jack or cheddar on mine.

Hot Burger Sandwich

Another option for the lonely burger I like is a hot burger sandwich whenever we have good leftover brown gravy.

Make the patty as in the previous recipe. Brown the hamburger buns in the Dutch oven, too. Serve open face with the gravy over it and whatever side dish you like. It will be a complete meal.

If you have gravy left over, this is a good way to use it. If not, it's worth making gravy. You can also use leftover roast for hot beef sandwiches.

Hot Beef Sandwich

If you have leftover beef or pork roast (even if it's little pieces with gravy), and some homemade bread, rolls, store bought bread, or hamburger buns, there are two ways to make a good hot sandwich.

The first way—mix the meat and gravy in the Dutch oven until as warm as you like, and then spoon it over the bread.

The second way—place all the meat pieces on the bread and then spoon the gravy over them. You can add chopped onion or cheese if you like.

Who said leftovers were not good?

Dutch Oven Fish Fillet Sandwich

Before we get to the actual recipe I want to tell you that I think everything tastes better in a Dutch oven. Even a sandwich can be surprisingly good.

1 fish fillet per person
1 slice cheese (optional) per fillet
lemon juice
⅓ cup bacon grease or vegetable oil
½ cup cracker crumbs — season to taste
1 egg per fillet—whipped

Dip the fillet in the egg mixture and then in the bread and cracker crumbs. Put the Dutch oven on a burner and add the bacon grease. When hot, put in the fillet and brown on both sides. Turn the heat down and add a slice of cheese if wanted. Cook until done and the cheese is melted—approximately 10 minutes depending on the thickness of the fillet. On the other side of your Dutch oven warm the roll, bun, or bread. When the fillet is ready sprinkle a little lemon juice on the bottom side as desired. Use a spatula to remove the fillet and the bread. Top with tarter sauce if desired and serve. I think you will like the flavor of your Dutch oven fish fillet sandwich.

Here again, if you are cooking outside, the directions will be the same. Use moderate heat so as not to overcook the fish.

As for the type of fillet, use the kind you like best. Also, if you buy the pre-breaded fillet (instead of regular unbreaded fish), don't double bread them. Some have good breading and I use them too, when in a hurry, but I prefer to bread my own. Enjoy them, whichever method you use.

Tarter Sauce

If you like tarter sauce and don't have a recipe, try this one. It's good on any kind of fish!

3 cups mayonnaise
1 cup sweet relish
½ cup finely chopped onions
juice of a large lemon
1 tsp. garlic salt
pinch of pepper

Blend it all together and you have 5 cups of tarter sauce. Keep it in the refrigerator. If this is too much for your need, cut the recipe in half.

Chapter Twelve

Dutch Oven Soups

Dutch Oven Chicken Noodle Soup

> 1 tbsp. chicken base per person
> 1 tbsp. black pepper
> 1 tbsp. salt
> 1 tbsp. garlic salt
> 1 tbsp. seasoning salt
> 1 tbsp. parsley
> 1 cup vegetables per person
> celery—chopped
> onions—chopped
> carrots—chopped
> ½ cup chicken per person, cooked, boned
>   and chopped
> 2 cups noodles—enough for 4 to 5
>   (homemade or packaged)

Select the size Dutch oven you need for the number of people you will serve. Add 1 cup water per person plus 1 for the Dutch oven. When the water is boiling add the chicken base, salt, pepper, garlic salt, seasoning salt, and parsley. Stir it all together and put the lid on. Get the carrots ready and add them first, letting them cook while you chop up the celery and onions. Then add these and let simmer while you bone the chicken and cut it into bite-size pieces. Add the chicken and all its juice to the soup.

While the soup is cooking, get the noodles ready. If using packaged noodles, cook them in a separate pan and add to the soup when done. If the soup needs more water, add the water in which the noodles were cooked. Mix it all up and let simmer until the vegetables are tender. Now it is ready to eat. You can serve it as a main course or before your dinner. It also goes well with sandwiches. Try it when you are in the mood for soup. It will take about 1 hour from start to finish, depending on how large a quantity you are preparing.

Dutch Oven Vegetable Beef Soup

> 1 tbsp. soup base per person
> 1 tbsp. black pepper
> 1 tbsp. salt
> 1 tbsp. garlic salt
> 1 tbsp. all purpose seasoning salt
> 1 tbsp. parsley flakes
> 1 cup vegetables per person:
> CHOPPED—celery, onions, carrots, cauliflower, zucchini, potatoes
> ½ cup pre-cooked roast beef per person

Before we get into the actual soup making, there are a few things I want to point out to you. If you can't eat salt, then be sure to use one of the good substitutes on the market.

If you don't like one of the vegetables listed, substitute another. When making the soup decide on the amount needed and choose the appropriate size Dutch oven. When figuring the measurements, use 1 cup of water for the oven, and 1 for each person. Use 1 cup of chopped vegetables and ½ cup chopped meat for each person. This will make nice big helpings for everyone. One last tip, if you are using fresh meat instead of leftovers, brown it first in the Dutch oven. Cook it for a time so it won't be tough. Don't remove any of the juices after it is cooked—this gives it more flavor.

Now that you know which size Dutch oven you want to use, put it on the top of the stove over the proper size burner. Put in the water and the seasonings, salt, pepper, season salt, garlic salt, beef base, and parsley. Bring to a boil and stir in the chopped carrots, then put in the other chopped vegetables and stir. Add the meat and juices when the vegetables are almost done, as the meat will turn to mush if added too soon. If you have a lot of juice from your meat it can be used instead of the beef base. Use it before it is made into gravy in order to get the beefy meat flavor. Use the gravy for stews or pot pies.

Keep the lid on the Dutch oven so all the liquid won't cook away. If you would rather, after all the ingredients are in, put it in the oven at about 250° until the vegetables are tender to the fork. Now it will be ready to taste. I believe you will enjoy it—we certainly do, especially on a cold day or night.

You can also add noodles to this soup—it will stretch it. See page 64, or use pre-packaged noodles. Also, as with the chicken soup in the next recipe, it can be made more special by pureeing the vegetables. This makes it a creamy soup, the kind served in many restaurants. Puree the vegetables when cooked and don't add the meat until after they have been put back into the Dutch oven. It is more trouble, but worth it. By adding water or taking the lid off for evaporation, you can make the soup as thin or as thick as you like.

Remember that you don't have to cook outside with a Dutch oven. You can cook on the top burners or in the oven of your stove. Just don't be afraid to try these recipes because they are made in Dutch ovens.

Everyone may not like soup, but I do and I really like its flavor when it's cooked in a Dutch oven. You talk about good! On a cold day a good homemade soup with a sandwich is a really great meal. Don't be afraid to try your favorite soup cooked in a Dutch oven— you might be surprised at just how especially good it tastes.

Dutch Oven Chicken Supreme Soup

This is my favorite homemade soup. It is more work but well worth it.

I have tasted variations of it in some of the better restaurants. I don't know exactly how they make theirs, but I will give you my version. I think you'll like it.

Before we get to the recipe, I want to give you some options. First, you can use any part of the chicken, not necessarily the whole bird. Second, the cooked vegetables can be pureed best in a blender, but you can also mash them with a potato masher. Last, use the vegetables that you like. Add these to those in the recipe at 1 cup per person.

Now for the recipe!

1 roasting chicken (2-3 lbs.)
1 tbsp. chicken base per person
1 tbsp. parsley
1 tbsp. garlic salt
1 tbsp. seasoning salt
1 tbsp. black pepper
1 tbsp. salt
1 cup vegetables per person (carrots, potatoes,
   celery, onions)
3-4 cups water

To get broth, cook the chicken in about 2 cups of water in the Dutch oven until tender. Use 12" or 14" oven on medium high. It will cook in about 1 hour. Then remove from the heat, and when cool take the chicken off the bone. Remove the skin, and cut the meat in bite-size pieces. Save the broth and chicken until ready to use for the soup. Keep it cool—sometimes it is better to do this the day before you want to make up a batch of soup.

When you are ready to make the soup, cut up all the vegetables and put into the broth and additional water, if needed. Add the chicken base and seasoning and mix all in a 14" Dutch oven. Now cook on medium heat with the lid on until the vegetables are tender (about 20-30 minutes), depending on the quantity you are cooking.

When the vegetables are done, puree them all in a blender or mash them. Put the vegetables and the boneless chicken into the Dutch oven with the broth. If more water is needed, add it now. Then mix everything together. Put on low heat and cook for 10-15 minutes. Give all the flavors a chance to blend together—it is now ready to eat.

If you want to make the soup the same day that you cook the chicken, the directions follow.

While the chicken is cooking, prepare the vegetables. Then when the chicken is done, remove it from the Dutch oven and add the vegetables (additional water if needed). Cook them while you remove the skin and bone from the chicken. Cut it in bite-size pieces. When the vegetables are pureed, add the chicken, the chicken base, all the seasoning, and water as needed. Then cook on low heat for about 15 minutes until all is blended together.

Use this as a main dish with hot rolls or hot French bread or as a first course of a special dinner.

I hope you like it as much as I do. It could be your favorite soup, too.

Chapter Thirteen

Sourdough for Dutch Oven Cooking

On pages 82 and 83 of *Let's Cook Dutch* I gave you the recipe for sourdough starter and sourdough cinnamon rolls. In the starter recipe a sourdough packet was used. Some people have written saying that they can't find any sourdough packets, so in this book I will go more into how to make a sourdough starter from scratch, plus give you some tips and a few recipes, too.

First the Tips

As I said in my first book, don't mix or keep the starter in a metal bowl or use metal spoons. Use wood spoons and a wood or crockery bowl. Glass is OK too. A lot of recipes call for soda. This will keep the sourdough from going sour if you don't like the sourdough flavor. If you like it sour, leave out the soda. If your starter turns orange it's OK—just old, but if it turns green discard it. The liquid will separate from the batter when it stands for several days but that's OK. It can be replenished if mixed in well, and it will stay fresh. If you are not going to use it for 2-3 weeks, freeze until needed.

Now for Starter

Dissolve 1 package dry yeast in ½ cup warm water. Stir in 2 cups of lukewarm water, 2 cups sifted flour, 1 teaspoon salt, 1 tablespoon sugar and beat until smooth. Let stand uncovered at room temperature 3-5 days. Stir it 2 or 3 times a day. Cover it at night. Starter should have a yeasty sour milk odor. Then it's ready so keep refrigerated until you are going to use it. To replace what you use, see page 83 of *Let's Cook Dutch* for keeping starter ready. If the starter is not used within 10 days, add 1 teaspoon sugar. Also it is better to have the starter dough a little soft rather than stiff, so be careful with the amount of flour used because of the differences in the flour, altitude and humidity. Practice makes perfect.

I love sourdough anything and I like it better when cooked in a Dutch oven. So now we will go into some of the other recipes.

When I wrote *Let's Cook Dutch* I didn't realize the interest in sourdough cooking was so widespread, and like Dutch oven cooking, more and more people are doing it and enjoying it. That's good. It is fun and we learn new ways to cook and new recipes to cook the old way.

Also, it is hard to find sourdough starter packets in many areas so I should have put more information into the first book—sorry for not doing so. But better late than never. So now you have the recipe for making starter and keeping it good. Now for more ways to enjoy it. You use the sourdough starter in all of these recipes.

Sourdough Bread

1 package active dry yeast
1½ cups warm water
1 cup starter
2 tsp. salt
2 tsp. sugar
5-5½ cups sifted flour
½ tsp. soda
melted butter

In a large bowl soften the yeast in warm water. Blend in the starter, salt, sugar and 3½ cups flour. Beat 3 to 4 minutes. Let rise until double—about 1½ hours. Mix the soda with 1½ cups of flour. Stir into the dough. Add enough flour for almost stiff dough.

Turn out on a lightly floured surface. Knead 8 to 10 minutes. Divide the dough in half. Cover and let rise for 10 minutes.

Shape into 2 loaves. Place on a lightly greased baking pan. With a sharp knife, make diagonal cuts across the top of the loaves. Let rise until double in size—about 1½ hours.

It is now ready to bake. If you are at home you can bake it in the Dutch oven. Leave the lid off. Put baking pan and all into your oven. Set at 400 degrees for 35-40 minutes. When done, take out and brush the top with butter when it is cool enough to handle. I like mine warm enough to melt the butter. Go for it!

If out camping, use 8-10 briquettes on the bottom and 30-36 on the top. I use a 16″. You might get them in a 14″ but it will be close. It will also take longer to cook.

You can see by the time it takes, it's not something you do without planning ahead. But it is good bread.

A few more hints. You can bake right in the Dutch oven and not use a baking pan, or you can bake it at home in just a baking bread pan. But I think it's a good idea to learn how to bake bread in a Dutch oven when out camping or in your own backyard. Just so you know that you can do it if you have to. If you like you can make 3 smaller loaves instead of the 2.

Don't let your companions eat all of it when it is warm or you won't have any left for supper or the next day. Come to think of it, maybe you had better bake 2 batches.

Sourdough Biscuits

½ cup starter
2 cups flour
1 tbsp. sugar
1 cup milk
1 tsp. baking powder
¾ tsp. salt
½ tsp. baking soda
melted butter

Mix the starter, milk and 1 cup flour in a large bowl. Cover the bowl and keep at room temperature to let rise. Add the remaining flour, salt, sugar, baking powder and baking soda. Mix with your hands and knead lightly to get the right consistency to the dough.

Roll on a floured surface to ½″ thickness. Cut out the biscuits with a biscuit cutter.

Set in a warm place to rise for 1½ hours, then dip the biscuits into melted butter, place in your Dutch oven, butter side down. Place the Dutch oven in your oven at 350 to 400 degrees for about 18 minutes until browned.

This recipe will make about 14-15 biscuits.

Now for camping—6-8 briquettes on the bottom, 20-24 on the top. Bake about 25 minutes. These are sure good! If there are any left, use for breakfast the next day. Here again, why not make 2 batches so you will be sure to have some for the next morning.

Sourdough Pancakes

1 cup flour
2 tbsp. sugar
1½ tsp. baking soda
1 beaten egg
1 cup starter
½ cup milk
2 tbsp. oil

In a large bowl combine the flour, sugar, baking powder, salt and baking soda. Mix it together, and to it add the egg, sourdough starter, milk and oil. Blend all together.

Spoon or pour out for the size pancake you want. Cook in lightly greased Dutch oven, over a burner or a campfire—medium hot. When you see bubbles and holes around the edge, turn them over. If it is not brown, leave for another minute or so until browned. Then turn over and brown the other side. This recipe will make about 24 pancakes depending on how big you make them.

For an added treat, if you like, add some crisp bacon, berries or nuts to the pancake batter. All are good for a change of pace. Serve them with butter, jam or your favorite syrup. I think that you will love these if you like pancakes.

Sourdough Scones

2 cups flour
1 cup water
½ cup starter
¼ cup dry powdered milk
1 tsp. salt
½ tsp. soda
1 tbsp. sugar
lard or vegetable oil for deep frying
    (2″ deep in Dutch oven)

The night before you want to fix these for breakfast, mix 1 cup flour, 1 cup water and ½ cup starter. Let stand overnight in a warm place. Then in the morning, add the other cup of flour, powdered milk, salt, soda and sugar. Mix together and knead well. Add more flour if needed to make a soft dough (up to ½ cup). Let rise until double in size—about 45 minutes.

In the meanwhile, put your Dutch oven over the right-size burner on high heat. Melt the lard so that it will be about 2″. Lard is better, but you can also use a good vegetable oil if you want.

When the dough is ready and the oil is hot, break off the dough. Form into the size scones you want and drop into the hot oil. When browned, turn them over and brown the other side. Take out with tongs and watch them disappear.

Scones are one of my favorite things to eat in the whole world of food. I could eat them with any meal. I have eaten them in a lot of places and have made them from all kinds of dough and never had a bad one yet. But I think that when cooked in a Dutch oven they are even better. Sourdough or regular dough, they have all been good eating. So when you want a treat, try them.

Serve with honey, jam or jelly of your choice. You will get rave reviews.

Chapter Fourteen

Dutch Oven Venison (Deer Meat) Section

A Very Good Combination

On pages 39 and 40 of the first book, *Let's Cook Dutch,* I told you about a combination deer and pork roast that is very good, and I still cook them that way. Now you can read about other recipes which use venison.

The reason for this section is simple—there are a lot of hunters and they often share their venison with people who don't like it or don't know how to cook it, and won't even try. I feel that this is a shame because they are missing a treat.

So you are about to read of some of the ways I like to cook and serve venison. Do yourself a favor and try these and you will see what you have been missing.

The first thing you must do is take good care of the meat. Keep it cool and clean, and remove the deer hair. Get the excess blood out by making sure the deer bleeds well. I always cut the fat off and bone it all except for the ribs. I marinate most of the deer meat, as I do most beef. It surely will not taste wild if taken care of properly.

Now for the recipes.

Dutch Oven Ranch Deer Steak

If you go deer hunting, here is another recipe for deer steaks that you will find very good and not dry.

1 venison steak per person
seasoning
flour
3 tbsp. bacon grease or vegetable oil
1 envelope dry onion soup mix
1 cup water
2 tbsp. Worcestershire sauce

Season flour to taste, then tenderize the steaks and pound flour into them. When ready, put the Dutch oven on top of the stove. Add bacon grease or vegetable oil. Brown all the steaks on both sides. Then add the soup mix, water and Worcestershire sauce. Simmer on medium (about 1 hour or until tender), adding water as needed.

This makes a good main dish. Serve with side dishes you like. If you have a friend that will not eat deer meat, fix this for him. He will like it and won't believe it's deer meat.

If your deer has a wild smell, soak it in buttermilk overnight, keep it cold, and then follow the above recipe.

If you cook this dish out camping, don't get it too hot. Remember, slow and easy.

Dutch Oven Deer Ribs

I have tried for years to find a way to cook deer ribs. Most of the time they are so dry that it is hard to enjoy them. Now I have a way for you to cook them—and they are good. You can also use beef short ribs when you have eaten all the deer ribs.

1 side of deer ribs (2 if for a large group)
1 lb. bacon (optional)
2 cups carrots—chopped
4 cups onions—chopped
1 cup celery—chopped
2 cloves garlic—minced

½ tsp. thyme
½ tsp. oregano
½ tsp. basil
1½ tsp. salt
1 tsp. pepper
2 tsp. chopped parsley
juice of 2 lemons
rind of 2 lemons
1 cup olive oil
4 tbsp. flour
1 cup consomme
2½ cups red wine vinegar

First we make the marinade combining the chopped carrots, onions, celery, parsley, thyme, oregano, basil, pepper, lemon juice and lemon rind in a large pan. Put in the ribs. Let marinate for 24 hours.

When ready to cook the ribs, take out the lemon rind and put them into the Dutch oven. Pour the marinade over them. Cook in an oven set at 250 degrees—total time will be about 1 hour for 1 rack. Baste the ribs with marinade often. Add 2 cups red wine vinegar after the first ½ hour, mixing in with the marinade. Cook until the ribs are done. Take them out of the Dutch oven and set aside.

Put the Dutch oven on top of the stove on medium. Stir the flour into the drippings until very smooth and browning. Then slowly add the other ½ cup of red wine vinegar and the consomme. Stir and be sure to scrape the sides of the Dutch oven for bits of meat, then mix it all. If you want smooth gravy, strain it.

Now cut the ribs into serving portions. Pour the gravy over the meat. I think you will like it—very tasty! In fact, you may want to try it on beef ribs, too. If you have a big deer, use the amount of ribs that you can eat at one time, or if you want to cook all the ribs at once, you may need more marinade. While marinating for 24 hours, keep the ribs covered and shake them up once in awhile so that none of them will get dry.

One last thing. As an option, I like to put strips of bacon on top of the ribs when I start to cook them. It keeps them more moist and adds extra flavor. So if you can eat bacon, try placing strips on top of the ribs while marinating. Don't wash off the bacon. You can cut a little slit in the ribs but the juice will come out. Better to use toothpicks if the bacon won't stay put. When it is cooked, chop up the bacon and leave in the gravy. That's the way I like it.

Now at last you can enjoy deer ribs and you don't have to cut the meat off them to make burgers.

Venison (Deer) Jerky

Jerky is a good snack, one I like to take along when we go fishing, hunting, or hiking, or when I just want something good to chew on. I think a lot of other people like it, too. So that's why it's in this section. Deer meat makes good jerky.

I will also give you some ideas for making jerky in the last chapter (Dutch Oven Cooking for Emergencies), in case your freezer is without power for a few days. Check that section for more information.

Now for the jerky. Cut the meat as lean as you can, ¼" thick and 2 to 4 inches long.

The marinade: this will be enough for about 10 lbs. of meat at a time. If you are making a lot of jerky, make a backup batch of marinade so that you can add it when needed.

Marinade for Jerky Venison
(may be used with other meat also)

1 gallon water	1 tsp. onion powder
½ cup salt	1 tbsp. garlic powder
1 cup brown sugar	½ tsp. tabasco
1 cup molasses	½ tsp. pepper
½ tsp. ginger	1 tsp. soy sauce
½ tsp. cloves	1 tbsp. Worchestershire sauce
½ tsp. nutmeg	

Boil marinade 15 minutes, stirring occasionally. Let cool, and then soak the meat in it for 1 hour.

Drain the meat and let dry on paper towels.

Place the meat on racks in your Dutch oven and keep the heat low. Use a 14" or 16" Dutch oven. The jerky should be done in approximately 6 hours. Put 3 to 4 briquettes on the bottom of a 14" oven and 12 briquettes on top. Use 6 on the bottom of a 16" oven and 14 on the top.

When you put the slices of meat in the Dutch oven, be sure they do not touch the bottom. The air needs to circulate to dry the meat properly. If you don't have racks that fit in your Dutch oven, use cookie sheets or aluminum foil. Use small rocks to lift the tray off the bottom.

If you are at home, you can make the jerky in your oven. Use the same marinade. Do it the same way except put it on cookie sheets and put on the shelves in the oven. Set on a low setting—it will take about 6 hours. When the meat is dark and dry, it is ready. You can eat it then or put it in large jars to save for later. I always need to eat a few pieces to be sure it has the flavor I wanted.

You can, of course, use the same marinade and method to make jerky out of beef, too. We make it because we like it for a snack. If you use good cuts of beef you will have good jerky. Try a batch just for fun and practice.

Marinade for Roasts and Steaks

4 cups water
1 tbsp. onion salt
1 tbsp. garlic salt
1 tbsp. Worcestershire sauce
1 tsp. black pepper
1 tsp. parsley flakes
dash tabasco (if desired)
8 bay leaves
1 tbsp. brown sugar

Combine all the ingredients. Marinate the steaks at least 6 hours. For the best results, marinate roasts overnight in the refrigerator in a deep pan so the whole roast will be covered. If it is too big, turn the roast over and spoon some of the marinade over it several times.

This marinade is also very good for any beef steak for which you may want to use it.

Venison Roast

venison roast
¼ cup bacon grease or vegetable oil
seasoning

Put the proper size Dutch oven for your roast over the right-size burner on your stove on medium high. Add the bacon grease or vegetable oil. While it is getting hot, take the roast out of the marinade and season to taste—then put it in the Dutch oven. Brown it all over. Turn the burner off, and add about ½ cup of marinade. Put the lid on, and set your oven at 250 to 300 degrees for a large roast. Put the Dutch oven in your oven and let it cook for about 1½ to 2 hours. Because roasts vary in size, watch it carefully. If there is no juice when you check it, add a little water and turn the roast over. When done the way you like your meat, remove from the oven. Use the juice to pour over the roast. That will be good eating.

If out camping, do the same way. Make sure the Dutch oven is level. Most of the heat should be on top of the Dutch oven. Don't let it get too hot. Slow and easy is best.

Deer (Venison) Steak

I am sure that some of you have had some deer steaks that were just fried in a pan on top of the stove. No seasoning, not marinated and overcooked, so they were tough and dry. No wonder a lot of people don't like deer meat. If I had to eat it like that, I would not like it at all.

I am going to tell you the ways I like deer steaks best and how to make them so that you will have a good steak that you can enjoy.

Marinate steaks for up to 6 hours

1 steak per person, ¾" thick
¼ cup bacon grease or vegetable oil
seasoning

Put your Dutch oven over the right-size burner on medium high. Add the bacon grease or vegetable oil. While this is getting hot, remove the steaks from the marinade and brown on both sides. This will seal in the juices. Now cook about 4 minutes on medium heat for rare, about 6 minutes per side for medium. If you want them well done, 8 minutes per side. Don't cook them so long that they get dry and tough. You will like them better medium done, as I do. If you don't want to brown them, first cook on medium heat for 6 minutes each side for rare, and 8 minutes for medium. Thicker steaks will take longer, and thinner steaks will cook faster, so be careful. Try to cut them all the same size. I like mine about ¾" thick cooked medium.

If out camping, the method is about the same. Keep the heat on the bottom of the Dutch oven and make sure it is level. Don't cook too fast with too much heat. Time will be the same—for rare, medium or well done, just watch them.

Venison Chicken Fried Steak

Marinate these like the other steaks, except that when you are ready to cook them, take each steak out of the marinade and pound with a meat hammer. Season to taste. They are not yet ready to become chicken fried steaks. I use two different coatings. Try them both and see which you like the best, or try combining them. They have all been good eating.

Milk and Egg Mixture

mix together: 1 cup milk
                 2 eggs

mix together: 2 cups flour
                 1 tsp. salt
                 1 tsp. pepper

1 steak per person
¼ cup bacon grease or vegetable oil
seasoning

This will do about 6-7 steaks. If you need to cook more, add ingredients as needed. Now put the Dutch oven on the right-size burner on medium high. Add the bacon grease or vegetable oil. While getting hot, take the marinated and pounded steak and dip in the egg mixture. Then in the flour mixture. Be sure the entire steak is coated, then put in the Dutch oven and fry until the coating is crispy. Then turn it over and do the same for the other side. When all the steaks are browned, put them in the oven at 250° for 15-20 minutes. When tender to the fork, remove from the oven and enjoy.

The Other Coating

mix together: 1 cup buttermilk
                 2 eggs

mix together: 1 cup bread crumbs
                 1 cup cracker crumbs
                 2 tsp. seasoning

Dip the steaks in the buttermilk mixture, then in the coating mixture. Cook as shown on the previous page. This coating is just a little different.

You can also use the bread and cracker crumbs with the plain milk, or the buttermilk with the flour. I have tried all the combinations—they were all good. So see which way you like the best. One thing you'll find out is that they are all good eating.

Chapter Fifteen

Miscellaneous Goodies or This and That

Special Seasoning

During the time that we had a Dutch oven restaurant, many of the recipes that are in this cookbook were developed. Also, a very special seasoning that was used in our cooking was created starting from a recipe that my son-in-law got from a friend of his. With that for a base, I worked on improving the formula.

After a lot of time and money, I was happy with the final product—it was worth the effort. So after selling the restaurant, I have been using the seasoning formula for several years. It makes all the food have a better flavor: fish, poultry or meat, or use it in your other cooking. It sure helps the flavor and taste.

I wanted to recover some of the cost of developing it, so I was thinking about selling it for $250.00—that was the going price for some cookie recipes. But the more we talked about it the more we thought that not many would spend that much for a seasoning, and we want it to be used because it is so good.

Anybody that reads this book can now buy the formula for $100.00—that way more of the people using Dutch ovens can afford to have it. You can even get a group of family members or friends to share the cost. That way more Dutch oven chefs will have it and I will recover some of the development cost.

As anything tastes better cooked in a Dutch oven, it also tastes better with this seasoning. Everything I have used it on has more flavor.

I use it now on everything in all my cooking. So if you want a special seasoning all you need to do is make out a check or money order for $100.00 to:

Robert L. Ririe or R. L. Ririe
Address: 105 Mallard
Las Vegas, NV 89107

Your formula will be sent by registered mail within a week and you can start to use and enjoy it.

A couple of final things you must know:

All sales are final.

The formula has salt in it so if you are on a salt-free diet let others try it and you use a salt substitute or don't use much of it.

So send your money in now before you forget about it!

Dutch Oven Quick Pizza

I like pizza even when I'm out camping. After a hard day fishing it sounds good, but it takes too long to make up the crust so I didn't bother with it because I wanted to eat soon.

The solution is some of the major supermarkets' pre-made pizza crust. It comes with a thick crust and in 2 sizes. The small size for 1 or 2 in a regular Dutch oven or a large one will fit in a 14" oven. Make sure you get the deep crust in a package that hasn't been frozen. Some of the frozen crusts taste like cardboard.

Another alternative to the purchased pizza crust is to use the fry bread. When this bread cooks up it is nice and thick.

Now, how to cook it:

I won't list the ingredients so that you can use whatever you like best.

First I take the large crust and pour on a bottle of pizza sauce or seasoned tomato sauce. Add the meat and mushrooms or whatever ingredients you choose, then cover with cheese. Put the pizza on a pizza pan and put in the 14" oven. Have about 6-8 briquettes on the bottom and 18-20 on top. It will take about 15 minutes for the cheese to melt. It is ready in not much longer than it would take to fix a sandwich, burger or hot dog and it sure hits the spot.

A few more tips to help you enjoy it more. If you don't have a pizza pan, don't worry, make one out of aluminum foil. Roll the edge down so that you can lift it onto the Dutch oven.

Remember the pan will be hot, so use hot pads or gloves to lift out the pizza.

Also, to save time have someone get the briquettes going first so whenever you are ready to cook, they are ready. If you are going to use sausage, cook it earlier and have it ready to put on the pizza.

These are some of my favorite things to put on my pizza: sausage, ground round, Canadian bacon, pepperoni, onions, fresh mushrooms, black olives, all kinds of cheese.

So if you like pizza, on your next camping trip try this easy recipe and enjoy.

Dutch Oven Quick French Bread

This is a very good side dish and it's new. It has only been out for less than a year or so and we have it all the time. It's good and quick, so look in the supermarket for all the tubes of rolls, etc., and find the rolls of French bread. Take them on a camping trip.

Just hit the end and the package comes open. Take out the loaf. Then in your Dutch oven, grease the bottom with vegetable oil or butter and lay the loaf in and slice the top in 3 places. Put the lid on the Dutch oven.

Put 4 briquettes on the bottom and 15 or so on the top. When it's golden brown it will be ready—about 20-25 minutes. But watch out—it is hot. Use gloves or hot pads to take it out.

Be prepared to bake more than one. Each package makes 1 loaf. You can fix them at home and cook them on a cookie sheet if you like. Just follow the setting on the package, but do try it.

A special bread to go with any special Dutch oven meal.

Dutch Oven Stuffed Baked Potato

I really enjoy baked potatoes. When I think about all the interest in stuffing them with all the good things that are available and all the potato bars around—people are doing now what I have been doing for a long while.

Whether you have any leftovers or just bake them so that you can try them this way, I think you'll really enjoy them.

When you bake potatoes for dinner, make extra so that you will have some to take out camping.

    1 baked potato per person
    shredded cheese
    bacon bits (cooked bacon crumpled up)
    optional vegetables you like
    cauliflower or broccoli
    1 square butter or margarine
    1 cup sour cream

Take the baked potato and slice it down the middle. Spoon out the inside and mash up. Season to taste and spoon back in the potato shell. Make a small pocket in the center and fill with the cheese and bacon bits.

Put them on the rack in the Dutch oven. This will keep it off the bottom of the oven so that it won't burn. But heat slowly with the lid on until the inside of the potato is hot and the cheese is melted. Serve with sour cream and butter.

Options: If you like vegetables in your baked potato, cook them first. Then add them to the potatoes with the cheese and bacon bits over them.

For a complete meal, serve them covered with chili as a special treat. They can also be served to complement any main dish you fix.

Dutch Oven Potato Patties

For a special side dish, I love potato patties cooked in a Dutch oven. If you have leftover baked or boiled potatoes, try them like this. Then you will want to have leftovers available so that you can have this recipe more often.

    5-6 medium potatoes
    3 tsp. butter or margarine
    ¼ cup sour cream
    1½ tsp. chopped parsley
    3 green onions—chopped
    flour
    2 tbsp. bacon grease

Take the skins off the potatoes. If you don't have any that are cooked, boil some in water or bake until done. After they are cooked and the skin is off, beat in the butter and sour cream. Add the parsley and chopped green onions. Now form into patties and sprinkle with flour (both sides) and they are ready to cook.

Put the Dutch oven on top of the stove on medium heat. Add bacon grease or vegetable oil. When hot, put in the potato patties. Brown on both sides until crusty brown.

Now you will have a very good side dish that is not hard to make and has a good flavor. It will go with breakfast or any main dishes for which you want something different.

Chapter Sixteen

Complementary Side Dishes

In this section I want to pass along to you a good recipe for a salad that I like to eat with Dutch oven food. Also, some dips and a salmon or cheese ball that go well with the Dutch oven as appetizers, or any time that you want a good snack. They come in handy during the holiday season or at special get-togethers of family or friends. When you want a little something out of the ordinary to nibble on, try these, and also the other good appetizers and dips in the appetizer section.

I hope you enjoy them—we do.

Salmon Ball

1 8 oz. can salmon
1 8 oz. package cream cheese
2 tsp. lemon juice
1 tsp. horseradish
1 tsp. finely chopped onion
1 tsp. parsley flakes
½ cup finely chopped walnuts or pecans

Have the cream cheese at room temperature. Then mix all the ingredients together, except for the nuts. Chill until workable, then roll into a ball and roll it in the chopped nuts until completely covered. Serve with crackers of your choice.

Cheese Ball

1 8 oz. package cream cheese
6 oz. blue cheese
3 oz. Roquefort cheese
3 oz. grated cheddar
½ cup finely chopped pecans
2 tbsp. soft butter
½ tsp. garlic powder
¼ tsp. onion salt
¼ tsp. Worcestershire sauce

Let the cheeses stand at room temperature until soft. Mix together with the seasonings and butter. Form into a ball and roll in the chopped pecans. Chill for several hours. Serve with your favorite snack crackers or chips.

Macaroni, Crab and Shrimp Salad

One of my favorite salads as a side dish, or alone.

1 lb. imitation crab meat
2 packages small frozen shrimp
3 cups cooked salad macaroni
mayonnaise
1 tsp. garlic salt
1 tsp. onion salt
1 tsp. black pepper

Cook 3 cups of macaroni while you defrost the shrimp. Put the cooked macaroni in a large salad bowl and let cool. Then add the shrimp and crab meat. Blend in mayonnaise to your taste. Sprinkle with the garlic, onion salt and black pepper. Blend it well.

This is a good salad. It goes with almost any main dish or with rolls or French bread. Serves 4-5 nicely, and can be a complete meal. If you have hungry guests, increase as needed.

Clam Dip

1 can minced clams—drained
1 pkg. soft cream cheese
dash onion salt

For another good dip, open a can of minced clams and drain. Mix them into 1 large package of soft cream cheese and a little onion salt. Serve with crackers or dip chips for some really good snacking.

When you have company drop in, fix the dip and appetizers of your choice.

Onion Cream Cheese Dip

If you like cream cheese and onion flavor, try this for a good dip.

Use 1 large package of soft cream cheese and mix in 1 package of dry French onion or onion soup mix. This is simple but good.

Spread on crackers or use the dip chips of your choice. It is also good in celery sticks.

Chapter Seventeen

Dutch Oven Cooking for Emergencies

Some church groups and others have advised each family to have a 72-hour emergency kit ready in case they have to evacuate their home because of floods, earthquakes, forest fires or other emergencies.

This should include all that you will need to survive for a minimum of 72 hours (3 days) if necessary. Now, I don't want to get into listing all the things you will need, but there are a lot of them. What I do want to do is give you some tips about emergency food and how to cook it. It should be as compact as possible.

Include 2 sizes of Dutch ovens depending on the size of your family. I think a 12″ and 14″ would be the best choice in the event there are others that need help.

Whenever I go on a camping trip, the only things I take to cook in are Dutch ovens. If you don't need saucepans, frying pans, grills, etc., it saves time and space. The space saved will be important when putting a kit into a limited area.

Most of you know how to cook in your Dutch oven, but what I want to tell you is how to use your Dutch oven lid as a frying pan separate from the bottom part. Look at the lid—it is slightly sloped from the outside edge toward the center. I thought everybody knew that, but at a lot of seminars on Dutch oven cooking that I do, some people are surprised at this.

What I have been doing for years, as the picture in *Let's Cook Dutch* shows, is to put 2 bricks or rocks on the edge of the lid and make sure it is level. Now you can put the coals or briquettes under it. When it is hot, place bacon around the outside edge. The grease will run to the center where you can cook eggs any way that you like them. It makes great omelets. Or you can use the lid on which to cook hot cakes. A 14″ lid will cook several small ones or you can make one large one. You can also use the bottom of the Dutch oven as a frying pan. Using the lid in addition will double your cooking area.

You can also, with bacon around the outside edge of the oven lid, cook up great hash brown potatoes in the center. You will get enough grease from the bacon strips to keep them from burning and they will have extra flavor.

Now, if you run out of bacon or didn't have any in your kit, not to worry. Just be sure you do take butter, margarine, or vegetable oil. You will still be able to cook the pancakes, French toast, omelets, eggs, or whatever you like. The important thing is that now you can double the cooking area with your oven when it is not necessary to have the lid on it.

I have tried this in a lot of ways and never had a bad meal yet. So much for the lid. Now let's think about good meals using the whole oven.

Remember, you are not now trying for gourmet meals, but to survive and have something that tastes good and fills you up.

One of the best recipes will be a stew made with whatever you have. You should have beef bouillon cubes in your food kit so that they will flavor your stew even if you don't have meat to put in it. With the bouillon cubes you can add only vegetables and still have a tasty meal.

Another good item to include would be a biscuit mix that mixes with water. Cover the stew with biscuits and cook until they are brown. This will add a little extra to the meal.

You can also use a good canned stew or some of the canned soups like beef and vegetable beef, then top with biscuits. You can add macaroni to stretch the food. Canned vegetables can be used, too—green beans, corn, etc.

If you don't want to top the stew or soup with biscuits, cook the biscuits in the other oven and eat with the soup or stew. If you cook the biscuits separately and they are not all eaten with the stew, they would be good in the morning for breakfast. Cut them in half and butter them. Brown in the Dutch oven until the butter melts. You can use the lid and the Dutch oven to heat these biscuits. Serve them with jam and hot chocolate that can be mixed with water and you have a good quick breakfast.

Now a few other ideas—you can also take along the soup mixes. There are several brands on the market that I have tried. The one I like best is the chicken noodle. Add a little rice and serve with hot biscuits—it is a good filling meal. To make it go farther add macaroni and extra water. This would allow you to share with others who may not be so well prepared. It would be very hard to enjoy a meal if others were going without. Add a little water and whatever else is needed to the soup to give them a hot meal. Just because they were not ready for an emergency, do not let them go hungry. So you share and eat a little less, but you feel good inside.

For some other ideas in case you get tired of soups and stew, there are 4 brands of pouch dinners that do not have to be frozen. You just boil them for 3-9 minutes. Plus a boil-in-the-bag of rice. If you don't have the rice, noodles or even old standby biscuits would go with the dinners and you can have a good meal. One advantage to these boil-in-the-bag dinners is that you do not have to worry about potable water in which to cook them.

Now that I have given you all these ideas and have you thoroughly confused about what to take and how much, I will go through a few sample menus to give you the basics with a list of items to cook, so that you can pick out what you like and what you would eat. You may have some ideas of your own once you get into it.

Another thought—some will think, why go to all this trouble when there is a disaster. Some agency will set up a camp and take care of all our needs. This might be true, but even so, it will take time for relief to come and take care of you. Perhaps up to 72 hours and you and your family can get very hungry waiting for them to get there and set up. Also, if it is only a small disaster (such as a forest fire or flood that concerns only a few people), there may not be any help sent.

I always think it is better to be ready to help yourself and your family and whoever else you can, than to wait for help that may be late or never arrive. If aid did come, you would be a help to them instead of one more problem.

We have a summer home in the mountains and go there as often as possible. Only twice has there been a fire in the area, but they were never close enough so that we had to move out. It did however, make us think about what we would do if a fire threatened us.

What I want to do is show you what you can do in an emergency if you plan for it and make it something that you are ready for—but hope never to have to use. Plan for short term emergencies as well as long term ones.

Your chances of survival are better if you plan. With the food listings and menu ideas, you can choose the items you like best, including the things your children will eat.

For longer emergencies add some extra items to stretch the

food. Try the items you select when on a camping trip and practice making up your emergency cooking kit—then use the items from it and replace them so they stay fresh. Add to your kit a little at a time and you won't miss the money as much. We got into it big time so that I could try out a lot of the items listed, but it might be easier for you to start with less and add to it each time you go shopping. That is an easy way to assemble your kit. Make up your list and buy what you can when you can.

For those of you with an RV, it will be easy to expand your cooking kit because you have a refrigerator to keep things cold. For those without a refrigerator, an ice chest works well if ice is available, or try to camp by a running stream which will keep things cool. If you have no way of keeping perishable foods cool, don't take them.

The lunch and dinner menu will be easy to have available for an emergency because most do not need to be kept cold. The soup mixes, pouch or tray dinners, packages of rice, noodles, macaroni, and canned meat will be fine at regular temperatures.

If you have a stream close by, use the water from it for cooking and boiling the pouch or tray dinners and save your potable water for drinking and cooking where the water is consumed or cooked into the food.

Also a supply of wood will help. So take an axe and use the wood for your cooking fire. Save the briquettes for when there is no wood. For a long term emergency or short term—if you have the room—a butane camp stove is a big help. This should give you some good ideas. Have a few practice runs and you will probably come up with some ideas of your own.

You can have some fun if you have children. Make it a game to collect the wood and to decide on the menu. By getting them involved you might find that they have some good ideas, too.

Breakfast Food List

Use canned goods as much as possible to avoid breakage and spoilage.

Short Term List

Pancake and/or biscuit mix, hot chocolate mix—add water, herb tea, margarine, vegetable shortening, canned honey, canned jam, pancake syrup (plastic bottle), cinnamon (small can), sugar put in a can with lid or sugar substitute, peanut butter, powdered milk, eggs.

Long Term List

For a long term list, combine the following with the short term list to give you a good start.

(Will need an ice chest or RV refrigerator), cornbread mix, bacon, sausage, cheese, packaged cereal, canned breakfast meat.

Breakfast Ideas   # Short term   * Long term

Dutch oven biscuits with peanut butter and jam or honey, hot chocolate, etc.

Dutch oven pancakes with your choice of hot drink
* With bacon or sausage on the side

* Dutch oven cornbread or muffins with jam or honey, hot chocolate, etc.

* Canned meat with eggs or Dutch oven French toast

* Side of bacon or sausage with hot chocolate, etc.

* Dutch oven scrambled eggs with bacon and hot biscuits, hot chocolate, etc.

Instant rice, with cinnamon and sugar and mixed with milk if desired

* Packaged cereal, at least 6-8 different kinds

Toast and jam if tired of biscuits or rolls, hot drink of your choice

* Dutch oven bacon, cheese omelet with biscuits, and choice of hot drink

* Biscuits and gravy

Let's go over each menu and then pick out the meals you would like from the list. Select the items you will need for the meals you chose. That will give you your basic list of food items to buy.

These ideas for meals will be for average servings for a family of four. You will know the eating habits of all involved and can judge accordingly as to how much to cook. Most small children don't eat much but teenagers can eat you out of house and home.

One last idea that might be of some help—in longer emergencies, try to combine with another family that you can share with. For example: if you have Dutch ovens and camping equipment with the know-how on Dutch oven cooking and have a family member or good friend with an RV who likes to eat, work out a co-op deal and help each other. If you get a whole group into the idea of planning, it will be easier to be ready for whatever comes along. It could also be a good chance to meet new friends.

Let's first cover the #1 breakfast menus for the short term emergency. As you will need eggs for pancakes, keep them cool and pack carefully.

Dutch Oven Pancakes
(using instant powdered milk)

2 cups pancake mix
1 cup milk (either pre-mixed or add powdered milk and water separately)
2 eggs

In a bowl mix the ingredients with a spoon until moist. Put oil, margarine or shortening in the Dutch oven you will be using and make sure it is level. Pour or spoon the batter into the hot Dutch oven—about 2 oz. each. This will make 12 regular-size pancakes. Cook until they bubble and the edges are dry, then turn them over. Cook until golden brown. Don't forget to use the lid of your Dutch oven for added cooking area. If you like, you can make about 20-30 dollar-size pancakes.

Butter and serve with jam or syrup while hot.

If you plan ahead you can use a pancake mix that doesn't require eggs or milk. This could make your packing easier—whatever you choose is up to you.

Now for the long term breakfast menu. For a lengthy emergency (more than 3 days), add the food lists together. If you have some way to keep food cold, take more eggs, bacon, sausage, plus canned meat so you will be able to have a bigger selection for all meals.

Let's first talk about one of my favorite breakfasts:

Biscuits and Gravy

Make the biscuits in one Dutch oven and the gravy in the other using the recipe in this book. Use some of the bacon, sausage or canned meat chopped up fine in it.

Start the biscuits first because they will take a little longer. When all is ready, cut the biscuits in half and cover them with the gravy. You can also serve the bacon, sausage or the balance of the canned meat on the side.

Don't snub the canned breakfast meat, it is good. I even fix it on sandwiches when out camping. Anyone that was in the service got very tired of this type of meat—I sure did, but it seems to taste better now. Maybe they have improved it, so don't be afraid to try it if you don't remember what it was like or even if you have never tasted it.

Dutch Oven Omelets with Biscuits

Make the biscuits using the recipe in this book in one Dutch oven. Then in a bowl, mix up 2 eggs per person and season to taste. Add what you have and like, such as bacon, sausage, canned meat, cheese, etc.

Put a little bacon grease in the Dutch oven and the lid. Pour ½ the egg mixture in the bottom of the oven and ½ in the lid. This will allow it to cook faster and make it easier to turn over. (If you have to use your Dutch oven to mix the omelet, you will have to skip putting bacon grease on the bottom. It will stick a little, but will still taste good.)

You can cut the omelet in pieces and turn it over or turn it over all at once. Cook until done as you like it. Serve while hot with biscuits.

Dutch Oven Scrambled Eggs

I like to cook mine in the lid with the bacon around the outside edge. I put the bacon on first and when it has cooked on one side, I put the eggs in the center and then turn the bacon over and cook until done as I like it. Stir the eggs while they cook and watch them so that they don't overcook.

Cook the biscuits in the other oven and when done, serve all together.

Canned Breakfast Meat with Eggs

These cook like the scrambled eggs with bacon except that this time, slice the canned meat about ½" thick and cook it on the outside of the lid. When one side of the meat is cooked add the eggs to the center—then turn over the meat. Be sure to check your eggs, they can be scrambled, sunny side up, over easy or any way you prefer. Serve with biscuits.

Dutch Oven French Toast

Make sure the Dutch oven is level and preheated, then put some bacon grease or oil in the Dutch oven and/or lid. Mix up several eggs with milk (if available) and season to taste. Dip the bread in the egg mix on both sides.

Cook the bread on both sides. This should be served warm and topped with butter, syrup or jam.

If there is any of the mixture left, it should be cooked as scrambled eggs so there is no waste.

Dutch Oven Cornbread

There are a lot of cornbread mixes on the market. I have tried several and they all taste good. So follow the directions on your mix— use 2 cups. Pour in an 8″ square pan with about 6 briquettes on the bottom and 18-20 on top of a 12″ oven.

This will take about 40 minutes to cook.

Serve hot with butter and your choice of toppings. Serves four.

If you get tired of biscuits, this cornbread is a good alternative. If you need to serve more than four, double the recipe and you can cook it right in the Dutch oven. Just don't let the bottom of the Dutch oven get too hot or the cornbread will burn. If you want to triple the recipe, you will need to use a 14″ Dutch oven. You will also need a spatula to lift the pieces out.

Now, last but not least.

Dutch Oven Hot Cereal

There are lots of brands and several kinds of hot cereal, so pick out the kind you like.

Let me tell you about one I like and you will get the idea and be able to go from there.

Rolled Oats or Oat Flakes

Boil 3 cups water and ½ tsp. salt. Add 1½ cups of oats, cover and let cook for approximately 20 minutes, stirring occasionally. Remove from the heat and let stand about 2 minutes. This makes 4 servings.

I like to add a little cinnamon and sugar or a good sugar substitute. It is sure good on a cold morning. Use your milk on it and serve with biscuits or cornbread if you want.

NOTE:

A word of advice—any time that you boil water in a Dutch oven, make sure that you wipe it and the lid afterwards until all the water is gone. Then cover all the inside with a light coating of vegetable oil so that it won't rust.

While you are outside you will have to protect your Dutch ovens from the elements, so be sure to keep them covered when not in use. Remember, take good care of your Dutch ovens and they will take good care of you.

Now, that is the breakfast food list and ideas for the meals. Let's review how to make up your emergency Dutch oven cooking kit for the size of your family and what they like to eat, or what they would eat if they had to. Make a list.

For Short Term (3 days) there will be at least 3 breakfasts. If there are 4 in your family and you select:

A. biscuits,
B. pancakes,
C. rice with cinnamon, the following is the food you will have to include in your kit.

1 pkg. pancake/biscuit mix
hot chocolate mix (12 packs)
    or other hot drinks of your choice
margarine
canned vegetable shortening

Optional: jam, peanut butter, honey
bag or box of instant rice
can cinnamon
sugar or sugar substitute
powdered milk
pancake syrup
eggs—if using pancake mix requiring them

Pack the items on this list in a chest except for the margarine and eggs, as you usually have them on hand and they wouldn't keep stored in a box. This will get you started and more can be added from the list for long-term emergencies for your extended menu. These additional items should be packed as well. You can use items from your kit to keep them fresh, but be sure to replace them or you will be out of luck when the emergency comes.

Keep an inventory of your kit so that you will know what you have in it. This should be done for the lunch and dinner items, too. You should also have a plan of your menus to show you how to stretch them if necessary.

If you don't want to take fresh eggs, there are several egg products that can be used—they are in the freezer section of the grocery store. They will defrost in 12 hours and will keep for several days if kept cold. A package has 2 8-oz. cups—2 oz. equal 2 medium whole eggs. These eggs can be used in scrambled eggs, or for pancakes. Try them when you have a test run and see how you like them. They can be easier to transport than fresh eggs, but fresh eggs will keep longer.

A few more tips on the frozen eggs—you can defrost them faster if needed. Just boil 6 cups of water, take off the heat and place the full 8 oz. unopened egg container in the water for 30 minutes. It will need to be used within a week. Keep the unused eggs cold and in their original container.

Now for long term add more of the short term items plus a package of cornbread mix, cheese you like, a package of cooked cereal you like, canned breakfast meat, and *(optional)* bacon and/or sausage.

This will take care of all the items on the breakfast menu. You can now make up your food list and menu according to the size of your family and their appetites, and multiply by the number of days and you will have a good start. Do the same thing for lunch and dinner, but have the short term ready to go first. Store in a chest, footlocker, heavy box or large suitcase.

In case of an emergency, one person should be assigned the food box, someone else the extra food items from the refrigerator or freezer, and another the other items like Dutch ovens, axe, stove, etc. All these items should be kept in a convenient location that would be accessible no matter what the emergency. If you have planned ahead, you can be ready in 15-20 minutes.

Lunch Food List

Short Term List #1

Dry packaged soup, seasonings, drink mix, canned quick meals (see list for ones that you want)

Long Term List #2

Active dry yeast, flour, sugar, shortening/vegetable oil, canned meat to slice, canned tuna, canned chicken, mayonnaise, cheese, biscuit mix, beef bouillon powdered or cubes, chicken bouillon powdered or cubes, packaged noodles, packaged macaroni, cornbread mix, instant powdered milk, instant rice.

For short-term emergencies, we'll keep the lunch simple. For 3 days you can eat a good soup that you like with biscuits and have a good meal. You can also have rolls or homemade bread if you want to go that far.

Let's pick out the items from the list. The list can be expanded and if there are items you like that will keep well, feel free to add them to your kit. These lists I have made represent my personal preference in meals.

Dry Soup List

chicken noodle	tomato with basil
onion	hearty minestrone
Chinese noodles	French onion
golden onion	country barley
onion and mushroom	green pea
beefy onion	oxtail
potato	asparagus
vegetable	creamy chicken vegetable

cream of mushroom

Follow the directions on the soup you select. With some you add the soup mix to boiling water and some you put in cold water and bring to a boil, stirring every so often. One package of soup should feed 4 people without adding any stretchers.

The chicken noodle soup makes enough for 4 with 4 cups of water and 1 package soup mix. All you do is boil the water in whatever you have.

I like to mix 2 kinds of soup and add some canned chicken—perhaps chicken noodle and vegetable. You can try combining creamy chicken with noodle or beefy onion with potato. There are endless combinations. Just try the ones that sound good to you. I have never had a bad batch of Dutch oven soup.

You can also use canned soups, though they are more bulky. Canned soup can be used as a sauce over sliced meat or by itself. We will get into some recipes later. Now let's look at the canned soup list. There are some good soups here, too. It would also be good for children to help select the canned soup they like and will eat. If you were low on water you could use the soups that do not need any water added. They will be in a separate list noted below.

There are several brands, so watch for special prices. Whether the regular or chunky variety, you can store them for a long time if you rotate them.

Soup List
cream of potato
New England clam chowder
vegetable
chicken vegetable
turkey vegetable
bean and bacon
French onion
split pea with ham
vegetable beef
ham and butter bean
sirloin burger
steak and potato

With Own Juice
beef noodle
chicken noodle
turkey noodle
chicken with rice

Soup For Sauces
cream of tomato
cheddar cheese
beefy mushroom
cream of celery
cream of mushroom
creamy chicken mushroom
golden mushroom
cream of chicken
zesty cream of tomato

There are others, but I have used all of these in Dutch oven cooking. If your favorite kind is not listed, try it in some recipe and add it to the list if it works out.

In addition to canned soups there are canned meals that can be used in your kit. These meals can be for kids or anyone who is hungry.

A few of them are:
spaghetti with franks
macaroni and cheese
spaghetti and meatballs
beef ravioli
spaghetti
several kinds of macaroni products in the shape of animals, letters and numbers, all in tomato sauce.

Now for some sample meals for lunch. First for the short term simple meals.

Your favorite soup from the list (canned or dry), serve with biscuits and drink mix.

Just heat in your Dutch oven—if it calls for water add it, if it calls for milk, use the instant powdered milk. Don't get the Dutch oven too hot if cooking with milk and be sure to stir it once in awhile. If you have a camp stove it will be easier to regulate the heat, and will be less trouble than making a fire in the middle of the day.

For canned meals, follow the directions on the can. Heat in a Dutch oven until warm and serve with your leftover biscuits. Don't get the Dutch oven too hot—it only has to be warm.

For the long term emergency meals, we will get more involved with a bigger selection, mixing some items together and adding others to make them go further, like noodles, macaroni and rice.

You can also use some of the pouches or try items that are listed in the dinner food section. Some are complete meals and don't need to be kept cold.

Remember, if you plan on using canned soup and not the dry packaged kind, one can will give you only 2 or 3 bowls of soup. So plan according to your needs.

For long term, to have a change, you can make cornbread. I have had many good soup and cornbread meals.

Now for some menu ideas for long term:

Macaroni and Cheese with Meat Chunks

For 4 people, use 2 cans of macaroni and cheese. Add a 12 oz. can or smaller of the canned meat. I prefer the smoke flavored. It is best to put the macaroni and cheese in the Dutch oven on medium heat. Then add the cut up meat, mix together and cook until hot. This can be served with leftover biscuits. If you want the biscuits warmed up, put a layer of aluminum foil over the macaroni and cheese and then put the biscuits on top of it. Put on the lid and put a few coals on top. If you don't have any extra biscuits, you can cook more in your other Dutch oven.

Chicken Noodle Soup with Dumplings

2 cans chicken noodle soup or 1 pkg. soup mix
1 can of water (total) for the canned soup, or

4 cups of water for the soup mix

For dumplings:
2 cups biscuit mix
⅔ cup milk

Follow the directions for the type of soup you are using, canned or packaged. Mix it in the Dutch oven with enough heat to boil it. In the meantime mix up the dumplings. Mix the baking mix and milk until a soft dough forms. Drop by the spoonful onto the boiling soup. Cook with the lid off for about 10 minutes. Put the lid on and cook for 10-15 minutes with heat on top, until the dumplings are brown and done. This dumpling mix will make about a dozen. If you need more, add the extra soup and increase the recipe as many times as you need to for the dumplings.

This can be done with any other soup you prefer—just be sure to use ½ can of water instead of 1 can for each canned soup you use because you want the soup a little thicker for the dumplings.

To make sandwiches you will need bread and as your store bought bread will not last very long, you will need to bake it in your Dutch oven. If you have a recipe, try making some to practice. For a long term emergency you should take at least 2 bread pans along. If you don't have a bread recipe there is a good one on page 86 of *Let's Cook Dutch*. Make sure that you have both books in your emergency kit.

Now that you have made some bread, let's try out these sandwiches.

Grilled Cheese
(plain or with sliced meat)

As you would do at home, put sliced cheese between 2 thin slices of bread. Butter both outsides and put them in a warm Dutch oven. You can use the lid too, if needed. When brown on both sides remove from the oven and serve. You can add the sliced canned meat with the cheese. You will be surprised at how good this is.

Grilled Tuna with Cheese

1 regular can of tuna
sliced cheese
mayonnaise

Put the tuna and cheese between 2 slices of bread, butter the outside of each slice, and then put in a warm Dutch oven. Cook until brown on both sides. Put mayonnaise on the inside of the bread if desired.

This sandwich is good without being cooked, also. Just mix up your tuna with mayonnaise and spread on the bread.

Sliced Meat with Cheese Sandwiches

canned meat or corned beef
sliced cheese

A simple sandwich, but very good. Slice the canned meat as evenly as possible. The 12 oz. can should make 4 good-sized sandwiches. You will need to use the lid in which to put the slices. Arrange the meat slices into 4 groups. Brown on one side and turn them over, then put the sliced cheese on the meat and heat until the cheese starts to melt. Remove and put on the bread. You can put mayonnaise, butter or whatever you want on it. I also like to warm the bread in the Dutch oven. So try it the way you like best. Here again, it will be a surprisingly good tasting sandwich.

You can also use canned corned beef the same way. I like them both.

There are additional lunch menus that are also dinner menus, so they are listed under dinner with a note that they can be used for lunches.

Dinner Section

Before we get into the food list and menu, I want to tell you why we recommend the dinner pouches and trays. They are the package of the future—with a vacuum seal they don't have to be frozen or kept refrigerated. The shelf life is 6 months to 5 years. If you keep them rotated you can have a lot of very good dinners and they will not take a lot of room in a foot locker. You can pack enough packages to last a family of 4 for a long time. Wait until you see the variety available. We always have at least a hundred in the house and also lots in our summer home. With a camp stove and Dutch ovens, you will be all set.

Ten years ago when I wrote *Let's Cook Dutch,* these pouches weren't out and I had a few good ideas (see pages 95-98). Then the first brand came out and I saw the wisdom of the idea. New items are continually added, so it gets better and better. Now there are four brands on the market and maybe by the time you read this book there will be a few more brands with an even bigger variety. So much the better.

I am really into this, so now you will know why this chapter was included. It is my hope that it will help some people to survive an emergency. It has also been fun and I will keep trying other meals when they come out. I have tried most of those on the market now, and I have stocked the ones I like best. I use them for quick meals or to try out new recipes, but I keep restocking them so that I never run out.

Now that I've told you why, let's get to the food list. These are the pouch or tray dinners that I have enjoyed. Most will be 300-500 calories and the cost is $1.79 to about $2.95 each. This, of course, will vary from area to area.

(also used for lunches)

Lasagna Milano#
Spaghetti Romano#
Enchiladas Acapulco#
Lasagna with Meat Sauce#
Italian Style Lasagna with Sausage#
Spaghetti and Meat Balls#
Chicken Cacciatore with Fettucine#
Chicken Cacciatore
Linguini with White Clam Sauce#

Chili Con Carne#
Chicken Supreme
Chicken Breast
Glazed Chicken Breast
Breast of Chicken Acapulco
Szechwan Chicken
Chicken Fiesta
Chicken a la King#
Clam Chowder#
Shrimp Creole
Beef Burgundy
Boneless Beef Ribs
Beef Peking
Beef Stroganoff
Roast Beef
Swiss Steak
Beef Stew#
Salisbury Steak
Oriental Pepper Steak
Sweet and Sour Pork
Cabbage Rolls

After reading the list, I'll bet you are hungry. There will be other dinners not on this list but these are those that I like best. Watch the stores for special prices. I also keep my eyes open for new items. If you buy a few of those that you want each week when you buy groceries, your kit will build up and the cost will be spread out. One pouch or tray dinner per person for each meal can add up, but they are a very good way to be prepared for emergencies. They are compact, easy to fix and taste good. I have never had a bad packaged meal in a Dutch oven and I don't think I ever will.

Always take more food along than you think you will need. You don't have to eat it all, but if you need more, it would be difficult to buy during an emergency.

These dinners are good out fishing or hunting, too. Now that you are thinking about them, choose some and try them on your next camping trip. That way you will find out your own personal preferences.

When you try a dinner that does not have a side of noodles or rice, fix them with the dinner. We will go into some to show you what to fix and how to do it.

These are foods to go with the dinners.

Biscuit Mix
Instant Milk
Noodles
Macaroni
Instant Rice
Beef Bouillon
Chicken Bouillon
Box of Crackers
Drink Mix
Hot Chocolate Mix
Other hot drinks
  of your choice

Now we will get into some more menus. As all the dinners cook in boiling water, if you are using boil-in-the-bag rice, cook them together. The rice will cook in 5-10 minutes. The dinners in 6-9 minutes. Follow the directions on the package. If you are going to cook noodles or macaroni, cook in a separate Dutch oven. Just cook the amount you need.

Noodles (8 oz.) will serve 4.
Macaroni (1¾ cups) with 2 quarts water will serve 4.
Rice boil-in-the-bag—one bag will give 4½ cup servings.
Instant rice (1½ cups) in 1½ cups water makes 4 servings.

If you don't know how to cook any item, just follow the directions on the packages, except that you will be using a Dutch oven.

First, some simple meals you can also use for lunch.

Chicken a la King Over Biscuits

1 package of chicken a la king per person
2 biscuits per person

Boil 2 quarts or so of water in the Dutch oven. You will need enough to cover the trays or pouch dinners, boil 6-9 minutes. When done, lift dinners out with tongs as they will be hot. Slice the pouch across the top and pour over the biscuits. You can slice the biscuits or leave them whole. One pouch dinner will cover 2 average biscuits. Tray dinners—lift out with the tongs and open the lid by lifting the tab and pulling it diagonally across the tray.

The following meal is done the same as the chicken a la king, so follow the previous directions.

Chili Con Carne

Sprinkle cheese on top and serve with crackers or biscuits and a drink.

Clam Chowder

Add a pat of butter and serve with crackers or biscuits and a drink.

Beef Stew

Serve with crackers or biscuits and a drink.

Lasagna Milano
Lasagna with Meat Sauce
Italian Style Lasagna with Sausage

All lasagna is a complete meal. Serve with biscuits and a drink.

Enchiladas Acapulco
Spaghetti and Meat Balls or Spaghetti Romano
Linguini with White Clam Sauce
Chicken Cacciatore with Fettucine

All these are complete meals. Serve with biscuits and a drink.
All the remaining dinners on the list will need a side dish if you want to stretch them. Cook extra noodles, rice, macaroni or whatever you have. Combine all the pouch or tray dinners and spoon over the side dish. With careful planning you can double the meals from the package dinners if you have to.
Let's go into a few that I have tried.

Beef Stew or Chicken Stew with Biscuits

Now say that you have only 4 pouches of beef stew left and there are 6 of you. Don't worry. Take the Dutch oven, put in 2 quarts of water and bring to a boil. Stir in 1¾ cups macaroni. Stir to separate and cook for 8-10 minutes until done. Drain the macaroni. Now mix up 2 beef bouillon cubes or 2 tablespoons of the powder in 16 oz. water. In the other Dutch oven heat the packages of beef stew. Add the macaroni to the beef bouillon. Also add 1 package of Swiss steak or roast beef, and a can or package of beef soup or vegetable. Mix all together. When the pouch dinners are ready, add them to the macaroni mixture and season to taste.

Mix up a batch of biscuits and put them on top of the stew mixture. Cook until the biscuits are brown. This will feed all 6 people plus a few others.

If you have to feed only 4 and have 4 pouch dinners, just open the uncooked pouch into the Dutch oven and cover with biscuits. Cook until the biscuits are browned.

Now, you can also do this with any of the chicken breast dinners. Dice up the chicken from the pouch or tray dinner. You can use chicken bouillon (either the cube or powder in 8 oz. water). Then add macaroni and the creamy chicken soup, chicken vegetable soup or whatever you want. Mix up in the Dutch oven and top with the biscuit mix and cook until the biscuits are brown. Make sure that most of the heat is on the top.

Remember, it will cook in about 10 minutes. Don't get the Dutch oven too hot or the stew too watery. Both of these stews are very good and can cook up in a hurry.

If you are out of beef stew package dinners, let me tell you how to make the stew without them.

Take 1 pouch or tray dinner of roast beef or Swiss steak, cut the meat in pieces. Add 1 beef bouillon cube to 8 oz. water. Combine the bouillon and beef in the Dutch oven. Add one can vegetable beef soup or mix up a package of dry soup. Mix it all together in the Dutch oven and season to taste. Put the biscuits on top and cook until the biscuits are brown. If you need to feed more than 3 or 4, add macaroni, or 1 more can of soup with a ½ can of water.

If you want to use canned stew, there are several brands on the market. I have used them and they work very well. You can even add beef bouillon, macaroni, etc., to make them go further. If you find it on sale, buy it for your emergency kit. 15 oz. will feed 2, 24 oz. will feed 4, and the 40 oz. size will feed 6 with only a biscuit covering. Be sure to get the size you need.

Just remember to keep your heat on the top of the Dutch oven whenever you are baking something. You will need only 4-5 briquettes on the bottom to warm the stew.

With a good selection of the package dinners you can last a long time and eat good meals.

Now let's go into a few more ideas for meals and the side dishes to have with them.

Chicken Cacciatore
Chicken Supreme
Chicken Breast
Glazed Chicken Breast
Breast of Chicken Acapulco
Szechwan Chicken
Chicken Fiesta

One pouch or tray dinner per person. Serve with your choice of rice or noodles. These are from 4 different companies, and each have a little different taste. Cook the side dish you want and in the quantity you need.

These can also be served with biscuits, bread, or rolls and a drink of your choice. Don't be afraid to mix them all together if you don't have enough of any one kind.

Shrimp Creole
Sweet and Sour Pork

I love both of these meals served over rice. They can also liven up a soup or stew.

Boneless Beef Ribs
Beef Peking
Beef Stroganoff
Roast Beef
Swiss Steak
Beef Burgundy
Salisbury Steak
Oriental Pepper Steak

All of these dinners can be served with rice or noodles and some I have even tried with macaroni.

Remember to cook the side dish in one Dutch oven and boil

the pouch or tray dinners in the other one. Put your side dish on a plate and pour or spoon the dinner over it. These can also be served with biscuits or rolls and a drink of your choice.

The last dinner on the list is:

Cabbage Rolls

These are good with rice and are cooked just like the other dinners.

I think you can see that the possibilities are almost endless. By combining some of the dinners and adding some things to them, like macaroni, noodles and rice, you have a good variety. So use your imagination and be creative. You may be surprised at what you can do and how good it will be.

Now let's go through the emergency plan one last time. You have read the food lists and have menu ideas—maybe some of your own, too.

Short Term: For 1-3 days, make up a food list and menu of the items needed to survive for 3 days and a little extra in the event that it's longer. Select the food items and menu from the things you like best.

Now, if you don't have a chest, use a box or a large suitcase and keep the items available. If you use something out of the kit, keep a list so that it will be replaced. If you have refrigerated items, be sure they are noted so that they will not be forgotten.

Long Term: Prepare the same way but include more food. Have extra too, so that you won't run out—if it isn't needed it can be saved for another time. It will be up to you to plan the amount of food you will need—you know your family and also know what type of long term emergencies in which you could be involved.

Make up a food list so that you can keep a record of what you need to buy and what you already have. Try some of the packaged dinners on a camping trip or at home so that you will know how to prepare them and what you do or don't like. Replace the items you use and you will be ready.

I hope none of you ever have to use the Dutch oven emergency cooking kit, and only use the ideas for campouts, but the more practice you get the better prepared you will be.

I know that my family and I can survive a long time with what we have, and will even be able to share with others.

So get your Dutch oven emergency cooking kit together and practice your planned menu on a weekend camping trip. Get your family and friends involved, too. Have your kit perfected and ready, then hope you don't have to use it. But if any emergency comes, all the preparation and work will definitely be worth it.

Jerky for Emergencies

As an extra item for your emergency kit, include a jar or two of jerky. Make it from the recipe in the venison section of this book. The mountainmen and indians eat it all the time when on the trail. I am sure there were many times when jerky and water was all they ate.

In an emergency, some good jerky would come in handy. It keeps very well and is a good, nutritious snack. You could last quite a while with jerky and water.

You don't have to wait until you don't have power or gas to make some jerky. If you want to have some in your emergency kit, make it ahead of time and it will keep without refrigeration—then as you use it just make some more.

I don't know about your house, but we have trouble keeping it around. We snack on it all the time, but it is better for you than all the junk food.

Now that you are all hungry for some, let me tell you about what to do with the meat in your freezer in case the power goes out for a few days or more.

You know that if you keep your freezer closed, the contents will keep for about 3 days, and you also know that you don't have the means to make it all into jerky, so a plan is needed. If it ever did happen you can make the best of a bad situation with the ideas and planning given here so that you can do what needs to be done.

Here are some ideas that might help in an emergency:
As the meat starts to defrost, smoke what you can if you have a smoker—it will keep better. Then from the venison section of this book, make up a batch or two of the marinade and cut the meat up as needed to make jerky. While it is marinating, you will have time to get your Dutch ovens ready and your fire going.

The first meat to defrost will be on the front of the shelves or on top if it is a chest-type freezer. As it gets soft, take it out and cut it up for jerky. If you have more than you can smoke or make into jerky, you can cook it in a Dutch oven as a roast—cooked meat will keep longer than raw.

Then you can use it for sandwiches, soup or stew and that way use it all before it spoils.

Make as much jerky as you can. It will keep longer and you can just put it in jars to eat when needed. With planning and practice you will be able to do it. Better to think about it and plan what to do, than hope it will never happen. If it did, you would have no idea as to what to do with the meat in your freezer before it spoiled.

With planning you would at least have some good eating and some good nutritious snacks.

Hope this will help you get a plan for your household. May you be able to enjoy the ideas I have in this book, and I hope that they will be a help in getting you ready. Best of luck, and may it be fun for all of your family, too.